GROW YOUR
CHRISTIAN LIFE

InterVarsity Press
Downers Grove
Illinois 60515

*Fifth printing
under present title,
January 1977*

© *1962 by Inter-Varsity
Christian Fellowship of the
United States of America*

*InterVarsity Press is the book
publishing division of
Inter-Varsity Christian Fellowship,
a student movement active on
campus at hundreds of
universities, colleges and schools
of nursing.
For information about local and
regional activities, write
IVCF, 233 Langdon St.,
Madison, WI 53703*

Originally entitled
IVCF Guide to Campus Christian Life
*Suggestions for Further Study
revised 1977*

*Unit 1; unit 3, day 1:Elizabeth Leake.
Unit 2: Charles Hummel.
Unit 3, days 2-7; units 5-12:
James P. Johnson.
Unit 4: Paul Little.
Unit 10, days 3, 5: Paul Fromer.*

ISBN 0-87784-661-8

*Printed in the United
States of America*

Preface

If every student on every campus is to have an opportunity to accept Christ, we who know Him must be (1) willing to sacrifice, (2) trained in the Word and in witnessing, and (3) filled with the Holy Spirit.

No amount of persuasion can make us willing to offer ourselves, our time, our possessions to the God to whom we, in fact, belong. If the suffering, humiliation, and death of Jesus Christ for us do not move us to surrender, nothing can. Mastery by the Spirit of an individual life so surrendered to Christ is the work of God Himself. But much of the training in the Scriptures and Christian life can be accomplished through the effective use of written materials. IVCF publications exist for this purpose.

The first steps in training for godliness on campus are suggested in "Life with God" and "Living Out the Christian Life." Of course, there is much more to being a man or woman of God than you will find covered in these pages. But here are first steps.

Godliness on campus, or elsewhere, is largely a matter of personal character and witness. You should be able to accomplish more as a group than individually; yet even your group meetings will reflect the level of your own personal spiritual life and vision.

These studies are designed to give you a daily workout of 25 minutes of Bible study and 10 minutes of prayer. If you have only a half hour or so available for your Quiet Time, these studies will make that time more profitable. If you have more than a half hour to spend on a day's assignment, there is sufficient content in each one to make a longer period of study rewarding. Incidentally, all you need by way of equipment is a pencil and a modern version of the Bible.

Having worked over the material thoughtfully and prayerfully each day, you will want to share the results of your study with members of your weekly core group. In this sharing, you will not only help each other; you will find that the core activity itself becomes the springboard of your personal and group witness.

Remember, your goal is to give every student on your campus the opportunity to hear a faithful, intelligent presentation of Jesus Christ in the power of the Holy Spirit.

June, 1962
Chicago

CHARLES H. TROUTMAN
General Director
Inter-Varsity Christian Fellowship

SECTION I / Life with God

SECTION II / Living Out the Christian Life

SCRIPTURE READING / I John 4

"BECAUSE GOD LOVED US FIRST"

The God in whom you have come to trust is the God of Scripture. He is the sovereign Lord who speaks to men through His Word, acting in His creation and in history, involving Himself in the events and circumstances of men's lives. He is Emmanuel, "God with us."

It is God's purpose to bring men into a new life shared with Himself—into the enjoyment of the closest and most intimate personal relationship. But how can man rest and delight in nearness to his Creator when his first reaction to Him is fear? Since the entrance of sin into the world, our natural response to the living God is: "Who is able to stand before the Lord, this holy God?" (I Samuel 6:20).

But God is love. In His immense goodness, God Himself becomes our refuge from God. In His love, God gives us life in Christ Jesus. God demonstrated His love for us by sending His only Son into the world to die that we might live. In Christ, God himself suffered at the hands of men and for men—bearing the penalty for our sins, procuring our peace. It is this love which draws us to Him until "we come to know and trust the love God has for us. God *is* love" (I John 4:16, Phillips).

Love cannot rest until it is returned. So the God of love will not be satisfied till He secures our love. To quiet hearts still troubled by the thought of Him, He likens Himself to father, mother, husband, brother, friend, shepherd, dove, a hen with her chickens—to anyone or anything of a faithful, loving, and tender nature. So great is His desire to make us sure of Him. When at last we see God as love, there is fellowship with Him in love. This, in faith, is the ground of all acceptable obedience.

Here is the great discovery of the gospel: the infinite and holy God gives Himself to men as the Father in free, undeserved, unalterable love. He has a design for us from eternity, a good will which His power enables Him to fulfill. He has a delight in us in Christ, all cause of anger and condemnation being taken away (I John 4:10; 1:7–2:2; Romans 5:10, 11; 8:1, 33, 34).

"We love because He loved us first" (I John 4:19, NEB). Everything begins in the love of God and ends in our love to Him. This is what the eternal love of God purposes for us and brings us to in Christ, in whom we find the love that sought us out. From this constant, unchangeable love, no one and nothing in all creation can ever separate us (Romans 8:38, 39).

MAKING THE TRUTH PERSONAL

1 / Why is God to be feared? _WE ARE SINFUL; GOD IS JUST AND HOLY - COMPLETELY PERFECT._

2 / How has God made it possible for man to move from fearful withdrawal to loving response? _BY SENDING HIS SON TO DIE FOR US - SHOWING HIS LOVE FOR US, THAT WE MAY KNOW AND LOVE Him - THROUGH CHRIST._

3 / What explains the fact that, although God has given men such evidence of His love, even His children yet fear Him? _BECAUSE HE IS JUST AND CAN HAVE NO SIN WITH Him_

4 / What has God given us that enables us to overcome this fear? _His Holy SPIRIT_

PERSONAL REACTIONS / questions, commitments, prayer requests

SUGGESTIONS FOR FURTHER STUDY

TEXTS / Romans 5 and 8

4

SCRIPTURE READING / I John 4; Ephesians 3:14–19

If we are to have a close and creative relationship with another person, we must know that person. Our relationship is false if it is not with the person as he is, but with that person as we imagine him to be.

1 / Who is the Son of God? For what purpose did God send His Son into the world? (I John 4:7–10) *X, TO PAY, TO CANCEL OUT, OUR SINS, BECAUSE He LOVES US.*

2 / What facts do we need to believe about the Lord Jesus Christ? (vss. 2, 15) *X HAS COME TO EARTH AS MAN, AND X IS THE SON OF GOD.*

"TO KNOW THE LOVE OF CHRIST"

We begin to live in fellowship with the Lord God at the time of our conversion, when we come to Him in faith, recognizing that He is love. Our fellowship is not only with God the Father, but also with His Son Jesus Christ (I John 1:3; I Corinthians 1:9).

It is in and through Christ that God's love to us and our love to Him are communicated. Everything God is and has for us, He gives us in the Person of His Son. Paul speaks of God lavishing all the riches of His grace upon us in Christ Jesus (Ephesians 1:6–8). Jesus is also the One through whom we offer our love and worship to the Father.

Can we know God and ignore Jesus Christ? God's answer is emphatic: "No one who denies the Son has the Father" (I John 2:23. Compare John 1:18; 3:35, 36; I John 5:11, 12, 20). On the other hand, "He who confesses the Son has the Father also."

What are we to confess or acknowledge about Jesus Christ? I John 4:2 gives us one fact: "Jesus Christ has come in the flesh." That is, He is fully human. Our fellowship with Christ is with a Person who lived in time and space as we know them. It is with a Person as He is revealed to us—not with a figment of our imaginations. So the Apostle John early in this letter stresses the reality of the incarnation: We've seen this Man with our own eyes, we've heard Him, we've touched Him with our hands—and we *know* that "the eternal life which was with the Father was made manifest to us." The eternal Word became flesh and lived among men.

I John 4:15 gives us a second necessary part of our profession: "Jesus is the Son of God." He is fully divine, and His deity is as essential as His humanity. The Word who became flesh also existed in the beginning; He was with God, and He was God (John 1:14, 1). Thus we do not merely admire Jesus Christ as a great and good man, but worship Him as God of God. We are called by the Father into fellowship with His Son as our Lord (I Corinthians 1:9).

Here is the infinite wisdom of God: Christ, one with Him, and one with us, and one in Himself in that oneness, in the unity of one Person. So the mighty God was a child given to us (Isaiah 9:6), and that holy thing which was born of Mary is called the Son of God (Luke 1:35). Only so could He bear our iniquity. Had He not been Man, He could not have suffered the punishment that was due us. Had He not been infinite God, His suffering would have availed neither Himself nor us. As the Mediator crucified for us, Christ is the Friend with whom we have communion.

MAKING THE TRUTH PERSONAL

1 / What difference does it make to me that God's Son took on flesh and blood—that He became like us in every respect except sin? He knows everything, personally, that we go through.

2 / What difference does it make to me now, in my daily living, that my Savior is not only Man, but also God? Means I'm "saved", I also can have a personal relationship w/ God, God forgives me, I now can love Him

PERSONAL REACTIONS / questions, commitments, prayer requests

SUGGESTIONS FOR FURTHER STUDY

TEXTS / Hebrews 2; Philippians 2:5–11

SCRIPTURE READING / I John 4
I Corinthians 1:17–2:2; I Thessalonians 5:9, 10

1 / In I John 4, what relationship do you find between God's love and the

death of Christ? *God's love was made apparent to all*
in the giving + the death of His Son, Jesus Christ.

2 / In today's additional texts, what relationship do you find between

Christ's death for you and your new life in company with God? *obtain*
salvation through Y, living with Him constantly
day and night.

"BY THIS WE KNOW LOVE . . ."

Love has a strong emotional element, as we well know. But we distort the
meaning of love if we define it in terms of emotion only, making God's love a
matter of sentiment.

The love of God is creative, protective, healing, sustaining. It is personal,
intimate—but not sentimental. It is free and gives freedom; it neither forces
nor abandons, but draws us to Him (Jeremiah 31:3, K.J.; John 12:32). The love
of God is uniting, overcoming the cause of our separation at a cost to Himself.
It desires our good. To reveal and communicate this love to man is the motive
and end of God's creative and redemptive acts.

God's love is self-giving. It expresses itself in action—regardless of our
condition or response. "God shows his love for us in that while we were yet
sinners Christ died for us" (Romans 5:8, RSV). "God so loved the world that he
gave . . ." (John 3:16). ". . . the Son of God . . . loved me and gave himself
for me" (Galations 2:20). Though He was rich, yet for our sake He became poor,
that by His poverty we might become rich (II Corinthians 8:9).

It is in the death of Christ that we begin to understand who God is and what
love is. By this we know love: God expressed it in laying down His life for us;
and we ought to lay down our lives for the brethren (I John 3:16). So the sacri-

ficial death of Jesus Christ becomes the defining and determining force of the Christian life.

All that we are, should be, and can be as Christians has its source in that great manifestation of divine love: Christ crucified. At the foot of His cross we leave our sins to be forgiven, forgotten, forever removed. At the foot of His cross we accept the gift of His righteousness (rightness, right-standing) that enables us to enter with boldness the presence of the Father. This interchange of sin and righteousness remains essential to our fellowship with God. Only in continued communion with Christ—as the Lamb of God who takes away the sins of the world and as the Lord our righteousness—do we rightly evaluate His love and grace.

To take Christ's work out of His hands and credit our acceptance with God to an indulgent Someone-up-there, or to our own repentance or spirituality or Christian activity, is to honor Him not at all. Whether it be release from sin and guilt or relief from suffering; whether it be light or life or love or strength or joy; whether it be fruitfulness in service for Him—all are to be found in the Lord Jesus. And His desire is to have in our hearts that preeminence that is His in the universe—not to be jostled carelessly among other gods, but as our sovereign Lord to be first in everything.

MAKING THE TRUTH PERSONAL

1 / Am I depending on anything other than the death of Christ for acceptance with God?_____

_____

2 / What concrete effect does my experience of God's love and forgiveness have on my life now? On my attitudes toward people now? _The life I live; my commitments. Frustration, want them to know X._

PERSONAL REACTIONS / questions, commitments, prayer requests

SUGGESTIONS FOR FURTHER STUDY
TEXT / 2 Corinthians 5:14-21
LITERATURE / Robert M. Horn, *Go Free!* (IVP, 1976)
James Denney, *The Death of Christ* (IVP, 1964) Out of print.
H. E. Guillebaud, *Why the Cross?* (IVP, 1946) Out of print.

SCRIPTURE READING / I John 4
John 14:16, 17; 15:26; 16:1–15; Romans 15:30

1 / Since no man has ever seen God (I John 4:12), how can we know Him?

Holy Spirit

2 / What does the gift of His own Spirit (vs. 13) enable us to know?_____

Enables us to know God and love God — to claim everything of : about Him for ourselves.

"THE LOVE OF THE SPIRIT"

What is God like? We don't know exactly, for no one has ever seen Him. It is impossible for us to comprehend God by reason: how can the finite embrace the infinite? It is impossible for us even to imagine Him; if we try, we create something that is not God. The essential nature of Him who is, and who is the Source of everything that is, remains incomprehensible.

We can know about God only what He tells us and shows us of Himself. It is His own Spirit who enables us to know the things that are freely given to us of God (I Corinthians 2:12). He is the divine factor in all that restores us to and maintains us in the life of God. The Spirit enlightens the responsive mind and heart to see in Scripture the Man who is the image of God (Colossians 1:15). He assures us that God is like His Son, and that His Son is the vision of what God intends man to be.

Thus the gift of the Spirit of truth to be with us and to direct our hearts into the love of God is one of the great evidences of God's love. It is He who gives us confidence that we are now the children of God, in a relationship so close that we are actually in God and God in us.

The presence of the third Person of the Trinity is a gift we receive—not something we earn, not Someone we proudly possess. He is the high and holy God who inhabits eternity and the contrite and humble spirit (Isaiah 57:15). Like the Savior we know through the Gospels, He is our Guide, Helper, Strengthener, and Advocate—sent by Christ to live in us, controlling every aspect of our lives. In all His activities His purpose is to exalt the Lord of glory and to make us like Him (II Corinthians 3:18)—partakers of the divine nature (II Peter 1:4). So He opens up to men new dimensions of love and life, purity and power. Man begins to become what he is and will be: a new creation.

Like the Father and the Son, God the Holy Spirit is to be believed and obeyed. In faith we look to Him, worship Him, wait for Him. Remembering that there is no peace with God, nor joy, nor hope, nor comfort, nor strength except by Him, we are mindful of His great kindness, taking care not to grieve Him. So we know the love of the Holy Spirit and have fellowship with Him in love.

MAKING THE TRUTH PERSONAL

1 / Although God is always near us, He may become for us "the absent God" if our experience of Him is shallow. What is the role of the Holy Spirit in making God a reality to us? _Bringing God and ourselves together in our understanding_ What is our role in this process? _We're helped, taught, shown by the H.S._

2 / How do I think of the Spirit of God—as a thing, an it, an influence, a mysterious substance, a part of God? Or do I recognize Him as God Himself— the Divine Spirit who indwells and transforms the child of God?_____

_____

_____

PERSONAL REACTIONS / questions, commitments, prayer requests

How exciting to know I'm being transformed daily to become more like Christ!

SUGGESTIONS FOR FURTHER STUDY

TEXTS / Galatians 5:16-26; 1 Corinthians 12 and 13
LITERATURE / Michael Green, *I Believe in the Holy Spirit* (Eerdmans, 1975)
Leon Morris, *Spirit of the Living God* (IVP, 1960)
Gordon R. Lewis, *Decide for Yourself* (IVP, 1970), pp. 117-121.

SCRIPTURE READING / Isaiah 6:1–8; 59:1, 2; Matthew 17:1, 2

1 / Describe the Lord of hosts as Isaiah encounters Him. What is the effect on the prophet of seeing the King?_____

_____

2 / What had to happen before Isaiah could offer himself in service and before the Lord could send him to speak in His name?_____

_____

"THY WAY, O GOD, IS HOLY"

God, and only God, is essentially holy. Because the divine is holy, whatever belongs to God must be thought of as holy. His power is holy power; His love is holy love. Whatever is not God cannot be holy in an absolute sense. Any claim of such holiness for a person, system, or thing is idolatry.

When men of God speak of the holiness of God they express a sense of His majesty—of that unapproachable, undiscoverable Mystery that enfolds the universe, filling men with wonder and fear. They express also a sense of the awesome purity of God—His total apartness from sin and perfect righteousness. Thus Jesus Christ is described as "holy, blameless, unstained, separated from sinners, exalted above the heavens" (Hebrews 7:26). Whenever man sees the Holy One, high and lifted up, he knows himself to be "undone"—literally, "cut off"—because of sin.

The holy and the sinful are utterly exclusive. The sinful is what God is not; it is unfaith, unlove, unlife. Sin is moral disorder—an offense against the God of order, beauty, justice. Because all sin is against God, any sin breaks into our relationship with God. For the believer, this is the central characteristic of sin: it interrupts the harmony and continuity of our walk with God. Sin is disruption of fellowship—even, at Calvary, between God and God. At the foot of the Cross, we see sin as all that it is to the Godhead. We glimpse the cost of our forgiveness to the holy Son of God, who alone could be the sacrifice and satisfaction for our sins—He Himself being the sinless One who is sinned against.

The Spirit of holiness cannot dwell with iniquity, nor can the Lord and Giver of life dwell with that which violates life. God's love must eventually destroy all that would destroy His love. Judgment is an act of God's mercy whereby He refuses to allow disorder and death to triumph over health and life. And the judgment of God begins at the household of God (I Peter 4:17).

Although God imputes and imparts holiness to His people, we are never sinless on this earth. But increasingly we avoid anything that separates us from our Lord. Our desire is to please Him in that effortless, spontaneous obedience that is part of love for Him. We obey Him, confident that His will is perfect—and the will of One who loves us.

But it is not always easy or pleasant to obey the Lord our Holy One. Because we are sinful, there comes at times a separation of will and will, ours from His. Then we recall God's twofold promise to His people: "I will not turn away from doing good to them; and I will put the fear of me in their hearts, that they may not turn from me" (Jeremiah 32:40). This is a comforting fear, insuring our own happiness. When we fail in the love that freely fulfills the law, we can rest on God's great "Thou shalt not's," moving on in simple obedience to His commandments. "For this is the love of God, that we keep his commandments. And his commandments are not burdensome" (I John 5:3).

"Great peace have those who love thy law . . . give me life in thy ways. Thy way, O God, is holy" (Psalms 119:165, 37; 77:13).

MAKING THE TRUTH PERSONAL

1 / How is the death of Christ the final expression of divine judgment on sin?

---

2 / Have you taken God's view of sin to be your own?

PERSONAL REACTIONS / questions, commitments, prayer requests

SUGGESTIONS FOR FURTHER STUDY
TEXTS / Romans 6; John 15:1-17
LITERATURE / T. C. Hammond, *In Understanding Be Men* (IVP, 1968), pp. 82-85.
J. I. Packer, *Knowing God* (IVP, 1973), pp. 125-42.

SCRIPTURE READING / I John 5:13

> Matthew 24:35; John 5:24; 12:48; II Timothy 3:15–17; Hebrews 4:12, 13; Revelation 19:11–13

1 / List the objective facts about God's Word which you find in the verses above._____

_____

2 / In what way do you think God wants you to regard His Word?_____

_____

_____

"THY TESTIMONIES ARE WONDERFUL"

Fellowship with God implies two-way communication: by God to us and by us to God.

God made us in His image so that He could communicate with us, and in many ways. He speaks to us, for instance, in the beauty and glory of His creation; through the events and circumstances of our lives; in and through people; and by the written Word that leads us to Jesus, the decisive Revelation of God.

Next week, in the second unit, we shall consider some of the practical aspects of Bible study by which we may listen to God more effectively. For to hear and obey God's voice, to love Him, to cleave to Him mean life: ". . . he is thy life . . . therefore choose life, that both thou and thy seed may live" (Deuteronomy 30:20; 19, K.J.).

There is nothing quite like the love of God's child for His living and abiding Word. That Word is utterly essential to him: he lives, not by bread alone, but by every spoken word of God (Matthew 4:4). His heart stands in awe of God's words, rejoicing at them like one who finds great spoil, and loving them (Psalm 119:161, 162, 140). He abides in the Word, knowing its power to cleanse and guard (Psalm 119:9), to guide and free (John 8:31, 32). He recognizes the vital connection between obedience to the Word of God written and love to the Word incarnate, which assures the presence of the Godhead. "He who has my commandments and keeps them, he it is who loves me; and he who loves me will be loved by my Father, and I will love him and manifest myself to him" (John 14:21. See also vs. 23).

The Bible consists of sixty-six books, written over many centuries, by many authors of widely different personalities and backgrounds, in several languages. Yet it is one book, revealing one God; one view of the world and God's purpose for it; one view of man (highly realistic) and God's purpose for him; one way of salvation—Himself. The Bible teaches us what God requires of us. It shows us that the purest efforts of our wills to meet His requirements can neither lift us to holiness nor spare us from hurting our neighbor. It wakens in us the highest consciousness of life: the reality of God and the love of God for us, with us, in us.

How should we study the Bible? There are several possible methods or combinations of methods. By all means, we want to make use of them; but we'll seek to avoid making a fetish out of method. The quiet time particularly is not just another study time, nor is the Bible just another book to be grasped by the intellect. Our first purpose is not to master the Word so much as it is to be willing to let the Word master us. In that period of the day we set apart for the worship of God, our need is to be completely open before Him, looking to Him to guide us through His Spirit and the Word. God is life and light; He alone can lead us into His truth. That truth in all its dynamic and creative power is never divorced from Himself. The Giver is in the gift and is the Gift.

> Happy is the man who listens to me,
>   watching daily at my gates,
>   waiting beside my doors.
> For he who finds me finds life.
> . . . he who misses me injures himself;
>   all who hate me love death.
>   (Proverbs 8:34–36)

> Thy testimonies are wonderful;
>   therefore my soul keeps them.
> The unfolding of thy words gives light;
>   it imparts understanding to the simple.
> Thy testimonies are righteous for ever;
>   give me understanding that I may live.
>   (Psalm 119:129, 130, 144)

MAKING THE TRUTH PERSONAL

As I meditate on these verses from Psalm 119, can I offer this prayer?

PERSONAL REACTIONS / questions, commitments, prayer requests

SUGGESTIONS FOR FURTHER STUDY
TEXT / Psalm 119
LITERATURE / J. I. Packer, *Knowing God* (IVP, 1973), pp. 98-105.
John R. W. Stott, *The Authority of the Bible* (IVP, 1974)

SCRIPTURE READING / Revelation 3:20; Song of Solomon 2:8–14; 5:2–6, 16
Philippians 4:4–7; I Thessalonians 5:16–19
Ephesians 6:18; Romans 8:26, 27

1 / What is prayer?_____

2 / Do you pray?

"THE VOICE OF MY BELOVED!"

"Behold, I stand at the door and knock; if any one hears my voice . . ."

Always God stands at the door of our selves and knocks, waiting for us to hear His voice and move toward Him. Love that is outside would be inside. But the door must open from within. Wherever He is given entry, He comes willingly to share all our life as He gives us Life.

As we grow in friendship with the Lord Jesus Christ, in the knowledge and enjoyment of Him, His voice means more and more to us. It is pleasant to hear, painful to miss hearing, and after silence or separation, wonderful to hear again. Increasingly we long for our Lord to speak to us.

How incredible that our voice is also sweet to Him, that He desires to hear us! In fact the Savior seeks our face as we do His (Song of Solomon 2:14; Psalm 27:8), finding us beautiful for He has made us so (Song of Solomon 1:15, 16; Ezekiel 16:14). However others look on us, however we look on ourselves, His words are: "You are all fair, my love; there is no flaw in you" (Song of Solomon 4:7). We may come with confidence to the One who calls us to Him.

We come to worship and adore, praise and thank, ask and intercede. We come to speak freely to the One by whom everything is known. We come for cleansing to Him who died for us. We come to listen to Him even as we speak to Him, for prayer is conversation. We come just to be with Him, in silence, for prayer is delight in His presence.

Must our communion with Him include these elements of prayer in this or any other order? Of course not, not if our relationship is vital. Like any personal conversation with someone we love, it will be spontaneous and free, varying with the occasion, the need, the time.

Some people say that in prayer we must always delay in asking anything for ourselves; when we do ask, it must be for spiritual blessings—as though we were all spirit! They lay down prayer rules and regulations, such as: "Petitions for ourselves will always come last." Since when? We don't have to apologize to God for being men and women—He made us after all—nor for any human need. It was our own great need of Him that first brought us to Him. It is our recognition that before Him we are always in need of everything—that without Him we are, have, and can do nothing—that keeps us coming to the All-sufficient One. And how joyously do we worship, how faithfully do we intercede, without having first experienced the blessing of God's hand upon us?

In Him we live all our moments. He who is the God of the sparrow desires us to bring anything and everything to Him. The very thought of the Lord to whom we pray helps to guide our thoughts, purifying desires that need His correction. Letting any and all requests be known to God—to answer when and as He knows best—brings us near to Him, and it is in nearness to Him that we are blessed. Prayer is thus an alignment of God's will and ours, a coming to oneness with the Lord of life.

It is in worship and adoration that we most nearly approach self-forgetting. Many of the subjects we have considered this week are themes for this kind of prayer. Both the source and end of all worship is the infinite divine Life, the essence of God, the divine nature. Even when we think of the Persons of the Godhead separately—worshiping the Father or the Son or the Holy Spirit—we worship each One as He is identified with the sovereign Cause of all things, God blessed forever. We adore what is common to all Persons. In each act of adoration, all are adored.

In prayer we also praise and give thanks. We praise Him for all that He is to us. We are grateful for all He has done and will do. We thank the glad Creator for His world of shapes and sounds and colors, for all the delight and joy and laughter of life. We thank the Potter who shapes the clay for His use of sorrow and distress (Psalm 119:75; Isaiah 48:10; 63:9). The psalmist praised God for that wonderful work of creation—himself; for God's help and deliverance; for His mercy, forgiveness, and cleansing; for His gentleness and goodness; for His name and His Word; for His steadfast love and faithfulness. "Because thy loving kindness is better than life, my lips shall praise thee" (Psalm 63:3).

In prayer we also intercede. We draw alongside the eternal Christ, who ever lives to make intercession for us, asking for the needs of others. "Others" means more than family and friends; it includes the "all saints" of Ephesians 6:18 and the "other sheep" that He must bring (John 10:16). Like Aaron we bear responsibility for them on our shoulders, concern for them on our hearts. Such prayer, strong in faith, is participation in God's purposes in fellowship with Him. It demands love, identification with His interests, concern for His glory. It demands discipline and perseverance. It is spiritual warfare, to be fought in the strength of the Spirit and the armor of God (Ephesians 6:10–20). It remembers always that "all the promises of God find their Yes in Him," that "Christ is the Yes pronounced upon God's promises, every one of them" (II Corinthians 1:20, RSV and NEB).

There is a kind of prayer that asks nothing, yet asks everything. It seeks the God who is enough and rests in Him, turning back all loves and concerns into

His hands, knowing that nothing makes life right or beautiful but the presence of the living God. It sees the Lord Jesus as altogether lovely, wholly to be desired. It receives Him who is lovely in His Person; lovely in His incarnation—He who took on flesh and blood for our sake; lovely in the whole course of His life, receiving evil, doing good; lovely in His death, never more desirable than when He was taken, broken, from the cross, having carried away our sins and brought us to His Father; lovely as Lord, in the glory and majesty with which He is crowned; lovely as Head of the Church, in His mercy, love, and compassion, in His wisdom and power; lovely as the King who is coming to reign. Persuaded that He gives Himself in all that He is to be ours, it submits in everything to Him, to abide with and be ruled by Him forever.

> Thou hast said, "Seek ye my face."
>   My heart says to thee,
> "Thy face, Lord, do I seek."
>   (Psalm 27:8)

MAKING THE TRUTH PERSONAL

Make Psalm 27 your prayer.

SUGGESTIONS FOR FURTHER STUDY
TEXT / Psalm 84
LITERATURE / O. Hallesby, *Prayer* (Augsburg, 1975)
John White, *The Fight* (IVP, 1976), pp. 19-37.

Do you find reading the Bible as exciting as a letter from home? You eagerly open a letter from someone you love to discover what he has to say. The same experience is possible with the Word of your Heavenly Father as you study it day by day. This week you will have the opportunity to practice using the basic tools of personal Bible study that enable you to understand and apply God's Word.

SCRIPTURE READING / Psalm 19

When we view a fiery sunset and later see glittering stars in a black sky we become aware of the power and glory of the Creator. But we may wonder if He cares about us. Does God have any concern and purpose for our lives, and how can we know? Consider the answer of the psalmist and notice the difference between general and special revelation. While we learn much *about God* from nature, we only *know Him* through His acts and words in human history. Throughout Old Testament times God spoke in a variety of ways by the prophets; in the New Testament His Word comes supremely in Jesus Christ (Hebrews 1:1, 2). This revelation has been preserved for us in the Bible.

The Word of God comes in human words with the richness of varied literary forms. Although inspired by the Holy Spirit, the biblical writers have their own style and vocabulary; they employ prose and poetry, narrative and parable, literal description and figures of speech to convey God's message to men. If we are to understand this message and its meaning for us today, we need to apply the basic principles of literary interpretation. But as we do so we must also realize our dependence upon the Holy Spirit to illumine our minds and prepare our wills to believe and obey.

As you approach the biblical passage read it through carefully at least twice. Discover the kind of literature, and try to glimpse the broad outline before you study the paragraphs and verses in detail. Then you are ready to use the basic tool of Bible study—the question. A keen question penetrates to the heart of the subject and lays bare its meaning. Three types of questions provide the tools for Bible study: observation, interpretation and application. Used in this order they serve as lenses to bring the significance of the passage into focus.

1. *Observation:* Questions of fact usually begin with such words as what, who, describe, and list. Be sure to *observe* carefully what the writer *says* before you attempt to interpret it.

2. *Interpretation:* These questions may start with such phrases as why, how, and explain. They help in the discovery of what the writer *means*, the message he desires to convey.

3. *Application:* What does it mean to me, here and now? How is my life to be changed? These questions, often neglected, build the bridge from the biblical world into our own; they forge the link between study and life.

Each day the Scripture selection will emphasize a particular type of application to Christian living. Much of the Bible is in the form of history and stories of individual experiences of God. This week you will make friends with Moses and Joshua, David, Peter, and Paul, and you can profit from their successes and failures.

At the start of your quiet time ask God to be your Teacher. The Scriptures have been inspired by God, and they are able to instruct you for salvation and equip you for every good work (II Timothy 3:15–17). You will find it valuable to memorize one verse each day; when a key verse is not recommended select your own. Expect that each day the Holy Spirit will bring you a sense of God's presence and an attitude of obedient faith to His Word.

MAKING THE TRUTH PERSONAL

1 / As you read Psalm 19 again meditate upon the closing prayer. Write out your own prayer today._____

_____

_____

_____

_____

_____

_____

SUGGESTIONS FOR FURTHER STUDY
TEXTS / Psalm 119; John 1:1-14
LITERATURE / T. Norton Sterrett, *How to Understand Your Bible* (IVP, 1974)
John R. W. Stott, *Understanding the Bible* (Regal, 1972)
J. Stafford Wright, *Interpreting the Bible* (IVP, 1955)

What is your concept of God? A policeman ready to blow his whistle when you step out of line? A kindly old gentleman with a grandfatherly view of life? The most important thing about you is what you think about God, since by an inward law of the soul you tend to become like your mental image of God. Wrong thoughts about God will cripple your Christian living, for an idol of the mind is as dangerous as an idol of the hands. The passage for today shows God as He revealed Himself to Moses. Before you read, pray that God will show you something new about Himself from these verses.

SCRIPTURE READING / Exodus 33:12–34:9

Through Moses God has rescued the Israelites from Egypt and led them into the wilderness. Already they have sinned against God by refusing to trust and obey Him; yet God commands Moses to lead them toward the promised land. These verses depict the depth of Moses' relationship to his Lord.

OBSERVATION AND INTERPRETATION

1 / What requests does Moses make of God (Ch. 33:13, 15, 16, 18)?_____

_____

_____

2 / Why is God's presence so important to Moses?_____

_____

_____

3 / What is God's response to Moses' petitions (vss. 14, 17)?_____

_____

_____

_____

4 / List the things you learn about God from the preliminary statements of

vss. 19–23._____

_____

_____

5 / Describe the setting in which Moses is to meet God (Ch. 34:1–5)._____

_____

_____

6 / Meditate upon the attributes of God in vss. 6, 7. What do these words mean? What do they show us about God's relationship to men?_____

_____

_____

_____

_____

7 / What was Moses' response to this revelation?_____

_____

_____

APPLICATION

8 / Write down any new thought God has given you about His character and action toward men._____

_____

_____

9 / How will it affect your life today?_____

_____

_____

SUGGESTIONS FOR FURTHER STUDY
TEXTS / Isaiah 6:1-8; 57:15-21; 1 Timothy 1:17; 6:15, 16; Romans 11:33-36
LITERATURE / J. B. Phillips, *Your God Is Too Small* (Macmillan)

Have you ever faced a task that seemed impossible? Perhaps God has placed you in a position of witness or leadership on campus for which you feel unprepared. When God gives an assignment, He stands ready to provide the resources. You will find in your own experience that His promises are as reliable today as in the time of Moses and Joshua.

SCRIPTURE READING / Joshua 1:1–18

Israel now stands at the threshold of the promised land without a leader. The crucial battles loom ahead and Moses who led them for forty years is dead. Into this power vacuum God thrusts Joshua with a great commission and a promise to go with him.

OBSERVATION AND INTERPRETATION

1 / Find the commands and encouragements God gives Joshua in vss. 1–6.

_____

_____

2 / What basic promise does God make that establishes the kind of relationship He had with Moses (vs. 5)?_____

3 / God's promises have conditions. In vss. 7–9 find the *verbs* which spell out Joshua's responsibility in this relationship. (Note the place of the law of God in his life.)_____

_____

_____

4 / Describe in your own words the means by which Joshua is to have strength, courage, and success._____

_____

_____

5 / What is Joshua's response and what action does he take to implement his commission (vss. 10–15)?_____

_____

6 / What immediate fulfillment of God's promise does Joshua experience in his leadership (vss. 16–18)?_____

_____

_____

APPLICATION

Jesus gave a similar commission to His disciples. He said to them: "You did not choose me, but I chose you and appointed you that you should go and bear fruit and that your fruit should abide; so that whatever you ask the Father in my name, he may give it to you" (John 15:16).

7 / God has appointed you to be a witness in your university situation. What resource does God promise and what responsibility do you have in claiming it?_____

_____

_____

8 / What task of Christian life and witness is God giving you today?_____

_____

SUGGESTIONS FOR FURTHER STUDY
TEXTS / Jeremiah 1:1–10; Acts 9:10–19

How often do you say "Thank you" to God? It is so easy to take His gifts for granted. On the human level ingratitude hurts us; how much more serious it is with God. The Apostle Paul puts failure to thank God at the root of sin: " Although they knew God they did not honor him as God or give thanks to him" (Romans 1:21). Today with the psalmist's help you have a chance to express your gratitude to God for His gifts.

SCRIPTURE READING / Psalm 103

David was Israel's greatest king; he was also a musician and poet. His psalms are a diary of life in the presence of God. Success and failure, joy and discouragement, are recorded in these prayers. As you study this psalm, notice that Hebrew poetry frequently employs parallelism in which an idea is first stated, and then restated in slightly different words (e.g., vss. 1, 7, 10, 14, 18). Rather than magnify the difference between the two statements, look for the *one idea* they express.

OBSERVATION AND INTERPRETATION

1 / Look for the verbs in vss. 1–5 which describe God's benefits._____

_____

2 / In vss. 6–10 find all you can about the character of God._____

_____

_____

_____

3 / Vss. 11–14 give three comparisons. What does each one teach about God's relationship to us?_____

_____

_____

_____

4 / Vss. 15–18 present a contrast. What additional dimension of God's love is emphasized?_____

_____

_____

5 / The concluding verses focus on God Himself. How does David portray His majesty and power?_____

_____

_____

_____

_____

APPLICATION

Do you often wonder what to pray for and whether your prayers are heard? Why not let God speak first, then answer Him accordingly. A psalm can enrich our prayer life in this way: as we meditate on it the Word of God comes to us, and we respond in prayer.

6 / As you reread David's prayer of thanksgiving, list the benefits God has given you and thank Him for them._____

_____

_____

_____

7 / When you finish the psalm think of other blessings in your life and keep on thanking God for them._____

_____

_____

SUGGESTIONS FOR FURTHER STUDY
TEXTS / Psalm 34; Philippians 4:4-9
LITERATURE / A. W. Tozer, *Knowledge of the Holy* (Harper & Row, 1975)

You have thanked God for His gifts, but how are they to be used? As a Christian what attitude should you have toward your abilities and possessions? Jesus Christ answers this question in the Sermon on the Mount as He describes two ways of living. .It cost you nothing to *become* a Christian; it costs everything to *be* a disciple of Christ. His words strike a discordant note in ears lulled by a mood of easy believism. In the following verses your Lord gives instruction for Christian service on campus.

SCRIPTURE READING / Matthew 6:19–34

OBSERVATION AND INTERPRETATION

1 / What three illustrations does Jesus use in vss. 19–24? Why do you think He chose them to teach contrasting ways of life?_____

_____

_____

_____

2 / What kinds of treasure are your friends working for during college years?

_____

_____

_____

3 / What is God's attitude toward our need for room and board, tuition, and good marks (vss. 25–34)? What evidence does Jesus give?_____

_____

_____

4 / Read through the passage again and find all the verbs of command. List each command.

a / _____

b / _____

c / _____

d / _____

e / _____

f / _____

g / _____

h / _____

APPLICATION

The key verse in the passage is vs. 33. Read it several times and memorize it. The concept of the Kingdom of God is not static but dynamic; it is not a matter of geography, but of the active reign of God in the lives of His people. You seek first God's kingdom as you obey the commands of your Lord.

5 / Study the list of commands in question 4 and find those which apply particularly to you now. Write out in your own words any specific situations in which they are to be obeyed today.

SUGGESTIONS FOR FURTHER STUDY
TEXTS / Proverbs 3; 1 Timothy 6:11-21
LITERATURE / Michael Griffiths, *Unsplitting Your Christian Life* (IVP, 1973)

As Christians we want to please our Lord, yet there are times when we fail Him. How do we get into situations like this? What can we do to avoid temptation and sin? It has been said that a wise man profits from his own failures; a wiser man learns from the failure of others. Today you have the opportunity to benefit from Peter's experience of sin and forgiveness.

SCRIPTURE READING / Luke 22:31–34, 54–62; John 21:15–19

It is Passover Week, and Jerusalem is thronged with worshipers. Outside the Jews are plotting Jesus' death. Inside the upper room Jesus has had the last supper with His disciples and now gives them final instruction.

OBSERVATION AND INTERPRETATION

1 / What warning does Jesus give in Luke 22:31–34, and what action has He taken on Peter's behalf?_____

_____

_____

2 / What evidence of self-confidence do you find in Peter's answer?_____

_____

3 / Note the setting in vss. 54, 55. What statements are made to Peter and how does he reply?_____

_____

_____

_____

_____

4 / Find the verbs in vss. 60–62 that depict the action after Peter's denial of

Jesus. What triggered Peter's repentance?_____

_____

_____

5 / Reread John 21:15–19. Why do you think Jesus asked His question
three times?_____

_____

_____

6 / What evidence do you find that Peter was restored to fellowship with his
Lord as Jesus had predicted?_____

_____

_____

APPLICATION

Temptation is inevitable; what counts is how you meet it. Jesus Christ
Himself was constantly tempted and understands this trial. He also prays for
you when you have sinned (I John 2:1). "If we confess our sins, he is faithful
and just, and will forgive our sins and cleanse us from all unrighteousness" (I
John 1:9). Memorize this verse. When you have been forgiven, you are ready
to strengthen your fellow Christians in their temptations.

7 / There are many ways to deny Jesus Christ on campus. Write down any
way you are failing in your witness to Him by life or word._____

_____

_____

_____

_____

SUGGESTIONS FOR FURTHER STUDY

TEXTS / Psalm 51; I John 1

2 / Personal Bible Study

AN EXAMPLE
TO FOLLOW / DAY 7

By now you have discovered that the Christian life is a struggle. It involves temptation, trial, and sacrifice, but the muscles of faith grow strong through rigorous exercise. Today you will study the Apostle Paul's example in a letter written near the end of his life.

SCRIPTURE READING / II Timothy 2:1–13; 4:6–8

OBSERVATION AND INTERPRETATION

1 / Where is Paul as he writes this letter (2:8–10)? For what reason is he suffering?_____

_____

_____

2 / Paul claims he has fought the good fight. What elements of military service illustrate the Christian life (2:3, 4)?_____

_____

3 / In what way is the Christian like an athlete?_____

_____

4 / What principles of farming operate in Christian living?_____

_____

_____

5 / Describe in your own words Paul's expectation at the end of his life

31

(4:6–8)._____

_____

_____

_____

APPLICATION

A basic principle of Paul's ministry is stated in II Timothy 2:2. Notice four spiritual generations. Study and memorize this verse. Paul had no intention of producing dead-end disciples. He multiplied his influence by developing Christians who could teach others to teach others. The ministry of many a man

terminates upon his hearers. Does yours?_____

_____

6 / Write in your own words any way in which Paul's example stirs you to

new action._____

_____

_____

_____

_____

7 / Is there at least one Christian friend to whom you may give yourself as

Paul did to Timothy. If not, why?_____

_____

SUGGESTIONS FOR FURTHER STUDY
TEXTS / Nehemiah 1; Luke 10:30-42
LITERATURE / Robert Coleman, *Master Plan of Evangelism* (Revell)
J. I. Packer, *Knowing God* (IVP, 1973), pp. 20-28.
Helen Roseveare, *He Gave Us a Valley* (IVP, 1976)

SCRIPTURE READING / I John 1:1–2:2; 4:10–12
John 15:9–13; 17:20–26

1 / From the verses you have read above, what do you think might be God's
definition of "fellowship?"_____

_____

2 / When you think of "fellowship" as the word is used in your circles, what
comes to mind? What does the term usually suggest?_____

_____

INTRODUCTION TO FELLOWSHIP

" 'A new commandment I give to you, that you love one another; even as I
have loved you, that you also love one another. By this all men will know that
you are my disciples, if you have love for one another' " (John 13:34, 35).

The term "life together" refers to our love for and relationships with other
Christians. This human fellowship is intimately, inseparably connected with
our fellowship with God. It is a result, a by-product of our new life in Christ,
existing only because of that new life, only because of Jesus Himself. We belong
to Him *with* one another, and we belong to one another in and through Him.

Christians share a common life that begins at the foot of the cross. Regardless of who or what we are, or think we are, there we stand as equals. We
are all sinners, overcome by our own guilt, helpless without Christ, dependent
completely upon Him for His salvation. At the cross, we fall at the Savior's
feet, knowing that there is *nothing* in us that enables God to accept us. By His
grace only He does so, for the sake of Christ who came to be the propitiation
for our sins. Through faith we accept God's acceptance of us in Christ, and
even that faith is given to us (Ephesians 2:8, 9). At this moment of realization
we are safe. As Bunyan phrased it: "He that is down need fear no fall."

The cross of Christ becomes the great "low door" through which we stoop,
all false pride gone, to enter Life. From this point on God's purpose is that we
walk in the light with Jesus Christ, having fellowship one with another. If we
forget the door through which we came and head toward darkness, fellowship

ends. We walk together only as we walk *in His light* and *as sinners*, saved only and continually by God's grace. "The blood of Jesus his Son cleanses us from all sin" (I John 1:7). Thus bound together in Christ by the forgiveness of sins, we are united forever in Him.

What has our fellowship with others in God, and with God in others, got to do with "food, fun, and fellowship"—a concept found in Christian circles today? Just about nothing. "Food, fun, and fellowship" often ends by being mostly food, on the ice-cream-and-cake level, with some superficial sociability thrown in for good measure. *Fellowship-with-Christians-with-Christ derives from deep commitment to Him and His.* It necessitates honesty, humility, acceptance of persons as they are now in Christ, and costly self-giving. It requires prayer and thought, imagination and time. It demands Christlike love. It is love that only God can give.

But Jesus Christ commands us to love one another—even as He loved us. *This love is the badge of discipleship*, the witness to Christ which we can give to a world that does not know Him. The mercy God shows us, we owe to others. We owe them love even if they, also owing us love, give us hate. The unbreakable bond, the vital link between us, is not natural sympathy nor perfect compatability, but Christ-in-us. All of us have our life in the forgiving love of God.

How did Christ love men and women and children? He loved them freely and "to the end" (John 13:1), forgiving them, serving them, meeting their needs —physical, mental, emotional, spiritual—not for His own gain, but for their well-being and for the glory of His Father.

Although Christ spoke and acted on earth with authority, He was in His own words "gentle and lowly in heart" (Matthew 11:29)—the most approachable Person in all the world. How do we claim to follow the Perfect One while we in our manifold, endless imperfections are proud and pretentious, legalistic and demanding? He never violated the freedom of those about Him, even "for their own good." He served to free still further those who came to Him, for He never used His love to distort or manipulate another person. How shall we justify our tendency to regulate and dominate, our self-assertion and presumption, our ready intrusion on another's privacy in the name of friendship, our brash curiosity that substitutes for the love that waits, ready as He leads to serve another for His sake?

As Christians we trust God to forgive us completely for depths of sinfulness in ourselves we have barely begun to comprehend. How then are we self-appointed judges, always holding court, always writing up cases against other people? If we look honestly at ourselves, and remember what God in Christ has forgiven and forgives us—with what gentleness He bears and forbears with us—we'll come down off the judge's throne. There'll be no more throne and no criminal box. We're waiting for an apology? No, we'll forgive with or without apology, remembering that in any concrete situation the one who forgives is also guilty. Human forgiveness should always be mutual. But again, we owe forgiveness even to the one who will not forgive us.

Deep, genuine contact between human beings is possible only in a setting of honesty and humility, and it is only by loving that one comes closest to a human soul.

It is in God above all that man meets man. Until we acknowledge Him as our neighbor's Father, equally as our own, we do not really know God or His love. In Him the lines of all our individual lives converge without crossing. He has made our individuality as well as our likeness, our dependence as well as our apartness, that love may bind us in the strongest of bonds to Him. When we permit Him to rule us as His Body, we are most conscious of the reality of our life together; for it is in Him only, and by His Spirit, that we love genuinely, living with one another in harmony.

"Now there are varieties of gifts, but the same Spirit; and there are varieties of service, but the same Lord; and there are varieties of working, but it is the same God who works them all in every one" (I Corinthians 12:4–6).

". . . be kind to one another, tenderhearted, forgiving one another, as God in Christ forgave you. Therefore be imitators of God, as beloved children. And walk in love, as Christ loved us and gave himself up for us, a fragrant offering and sacrifice to God" (Ephesians 4:32; 5:1, 2).

MAKING THE TRUTH PERSONAL

1 / Are you satisfied with your relationships to other Christians?
2 / Pray that during this week your study of fellowship may enrich your own experience with others.

PERSONAL REACTIONS / questions, commitments, prayer requests

SUGGESTIONS FOR FURTHER STUDY
TEXTS / 1 Corinthians 12 and 13
LITERATURE / Wayne Roberts, "Christians in Conflict," HIS, Dec. 1974.
Ray Stedman, *Body Life* (Regal, 1972)

PURPOSE / To see how our relationships with other people are changed when we are made alive in Christ.

SCRIPTURE READING / Ephesians 2:11–22

1 / How did Christ's death change the relationship between the Jews and Gentiles who became Christians (vss. 12–16)?_____

_____

_____

2 / How has the death of Christ changed your attitude toward differences between you and other Christians?_____

_____

_____

SUMMARY OF TEACHING

Before the resurrection there was a strong distinction between the Jews, God's people by the covenant, and the Gentiles. Nationality, laws, ritual, traditions, promises: all these things separated them. But in Jesus Christ the distinctions were set aside, since Jews and Gentiles alike could have access to God through faith. In their new relationship with God they discovered a new relationship with one another. No longer strangers, they were now united: (a) as members of a family, the household of God; (b) as fellow-citizens in a kingdom, under God's reign; and (c) as interdependent building blocks in a structure, the temple where God lived in the Spirit.

Today individuals find themselves separated from God and their fellow men by countless barriers. But Christians discover that the death of Jesus Christ not only reconciles us to God but also ends our alienation from other people. Like the first Christians, we have been brought together by God. We are needed, accepted, functioning members of God's Church, where separating distinctions have been made void, and where together we must demonstrate in action the truth of this new relationship.

MAKING THE TRUTH PERSONAL

1 / List some of the barriers that keep Christians on campus from accepting one another._____

_____

_____

_____

2 / What specific changes have been made in your attitudes and behavior toward other Christians? Test yourself on these possible barriers: denominational issues, nationality or race, personal appearance, educational achievements, financial status, cultural tastes, family background, fear of being known personally, political viewpoint._____

_____

_____

_____

_____

PERSONAL REACTIONS / questions, commitments, prayer requests

SUGGESTIONS FOR FURTHER STUDY

TEXTS / Jonah 1–4; Colossians 3:5–11

PURPOSE / To see how practical unity with other Christians is achieved and expressed.

SCRIPTURE READING / John 13:1–17, Philippians 1:27–2:4

1 / What did Jesus realize about Himself before He washed the disciples' feet (vs. 3)? _____

_____

_____ Why did He do it?_____

_____

_____

2 / What basic attitudes did Paul want the Philippian Christians to have toward one another? Why?_____

_____

_____

_____

SUMMARY OF TEACHING

Although it is God who brings individuals into His family, true fellowship is not automatically produced there. Each member must work to maintain the unity and sharing of life that God desires.

Jesus pointed the way by dramatically demonstrating that His followers must be servants of one another, and that special abilities, position, and achievements do not excuse anyone from this obligation. Selfishness and pride have no place. Rather, we must reach out to care for the needs of others.

In the Church we come from varying backgrounds and possess diverse abilities and conflicting temperaments and interests. We must therefore cultivate personal relationships with one another so that we understand each other and learn to love in practical ways, developing mutual trust and concern. To maintain fellowship we must be honest, ready to share ourselves and our possessions, and willing to forgive each other's weaknesses and sins.

MAKING THE TRUTH PERSONAL

1 / Think through the relationship you have with other Christians on campus. In what specific ways do you show that you are their servant?_____

_____

_____

2 / How can you personally cultivate greater unity in thinking and action among the Christians in your group? Consider differences of opinion about recreation, dress, entertainment, methods of evangelism, fraternities._____

_____

_____

_____

Thank God that He has put you with others who can share all of life with you.

PERSONAL REACTIONS / questions, commitments, prayer requests

SUGGESTIONS FOR FURTHER STUDY

TEXTS / I Corinthians 1:10–18; Romans 14

PURPOSE / To see how Christians are to help one another in their life together.

SCRIPTURE READING / I Thessalonians 2:5–12; 5:11–24

1 / How did Paul demonstrate the ways Christians are to help one another?

_____

_____

2 / Among the instructions Paul gave the Thessalonians list those which are most meaningful to you._____

_____

_____

_____

_____

SUMMARY OF TEACHING

Because Jesus Christ has come to live in us, we can mediate His life to one another. He wants us to be "little Christs," ministering to others as He would. This is done in many ways (since it encompasses all of life), but the aim is to seek the other's good and help him on to maturity.

The Apostle Paul showed that it is costly to share ourselves by serving others. He also showed that it is God's way of winning men to Christ and helping them mature.

The person who learns quickly must help the slower person with his studies. When someone is discouraged, we should take time to encourage him. If he needs understanding, our friendliness can enable him to talk to us. We must be patient when others disagree or criticize us, and not strike back vindictively when someone hurts us. We must think of the good qualities in other Christians and thank God for them.

MAKING THE TRUTH PERSONAL

1 / Paul gives two pictures of his relationship to the Thessalonians (2:7, 11). In what way can the leaders in your group apply these examples?_____

_____

_____

_____

_____

2 / Mention one way in which other Christians could help you._____

_____

_____

_____

3 / In what specific way can you help another Christian today?_____

_____

PERSONAL REACTIONS / questions, commitments, prayer requests

SUGGESTIONS FOR FURTHER STUDY

TEXTS / Romans 15; Ephesians 4:25–5:21; I Peter 4:7–11

PURPOSE / To see how Christians are to learn from one another.

SCRIPTURE READING / II Timothy 2:1–2; 3:10–17; I Timothy 1:3–7

1 / How does Paul provide for a continuance of teaching in the Christian fellowship (II Timothy 2:2)?_____

_____

2 / What aspects of Paul's life did Timothy witness (3:10–11)? Which of these in your life can God use to teach others?_____

_____

_____

SUMMARY OF TEACHING

Some members of the Body of Christ are especially equipped by God to teach true doctrine, and they must use this gift wisely for the sake of others. But their ministry does not provide all of the teaching needed in the Church. Each Christian, as he learns from God's Word and from experience, can teach others. This is not merely a good idea; it is a biblical pattern that must be followed in order to provide instruction among Christians.

Jesus spent three years' time in public ministry, but used the bulk of it to train twelve disciples so that they in turn would be prepared to teach. He used every principle needed to train. He taught principles, explained them in private, gave illustrations, demonstrated what He taught by personal example, questioned the disciples, assigned them work, sent them to do it, and evaluated it afterwards.

The Apostle Paul used the same methods as Jesus. And he urged that those whom he taught should teach the truth to others who would also teach it. The Scriptures equip each Christian for every good work; they are the basis for teaching, conduct, and correction. We do not learn and teach merely for the purpose of speculation and debate. Christian instruction must produce character. "The aim is love that issues from a pure heart and a good conscience and sincere faith."

MAKING THE TRUTH PERSONAL

1 / Describe one practical lesson you have learned by talking with or observing the lives of other Christians on your campus._____

_____

_____

_____

_____

2 / In what ways are you involved in teaching other Christians?_____

_____

_____

_____

PERSONAL REACTIONS / questions, commitments, prayer requests

SUGGESTIONS FOR FURTHER STUDY
TEXTS / Hebrews 5:11–14

PURPOSE / To see the place of group prayer in the fellowship of Christians.

SCRIPTURE READING / Matthew 18:19-20; Acts 4:23-31; 13:1-3

1 / What was the place of prayer in the corporate life of Christians?_____

_____

_____

_____

2 / What were the results of their praying together?_____

_____

_____

_____

SUMMARY OF TEACHING

Jesus gave us the impetus to pray together by saying that He would be with us when we gathered in His name and would grant our requests. After Jesus' ascension the disciples and new believers united and devoted themselves to prayer. They were aware of their relationship as brothers in Jesus Christ, and the prayer meeting became a family meeting.

In praying together the believers worshiped the Lord, and expressed confidence in Him and in His power to work through them. They showed their unity in the face of a hostile world as they supported one another in prayer by agreeing together and asking God for help. When they discovered the will of God, they sealed their decisions in prayer.

The early Christians were particularly aware that they were involved in a great warfare, a spiritual battle. They saw that they must fight it with spiritual weapons, and they called on one another to aid them by fervent and faithful intercession, believing that God would work in response to it. They exhorted young Christians to pray constantly and call down God's blessings on each other and all men. It was through prayer that they could maintain the most intimate and practical fellowship with Jesus Christ and with one another.

MAKING THE TRUTH PERSONAL

1 / List the most important motives that have led you to pray with other Christians._____

_____

_____

_____

_____

2 / What should you pray about with other Christians?_____

_____

_____

_____

PERSONAL REACTIONS / questions, commitments, prayer requests

SUGGESTIONS FOR FURTHER STUDY
TEXTS / 1 Timothy 2:1-8; James 5:13-18; 2 Corinthians 1:11
LITERATURE / John Paterson, *How to Pray Together* (IVP, 1964)
Michael Griffiths, *Unsplitting Your Christian Life* (IVP, 1973)

PURPOSE / To see how Christians as a group are involved in the spread of the gospel.

SCRIPTURE READING / I Thessalonians 1:1–10; Acts 8:1–4; 11:19–26

1 / How did the Thessalonians become involved in evangelism after Paul left them?_____

_____

_____

_____

2 / Who in the churches were involved in witnessing, and how?_____

_____

_____

_____

_____

SUMMARY OF TEACHING

The New Testament teaches that there were special individuals in the churches whose whole energies were given to proclaiming the gospel publicly. God used them in remarkable ways to bring about commitment to Christ.

But the New Testament doesn't imply that the work of evangelism is the specialized function of a few individuals in the church. Because of the persecution after Stephen's death, all believers except the apostles left Jerusalem. Wherever they went, the rank-and-file Christians announced that Jesus was the Christ, and little groups of followers of "the Way" sprang up. The Christians "gossiped" the good news so that the truth was known widely, and their changed life and relationship with one another supported what they said. Again and again the impact of the gospel in an area came through the combined witness of all the members of a local church.

Also, local congregations sent their representatives in small teams to preach where Jesus Christ was not known. These men worked together closely in establishing churches which became centers for proclaiming the gospel in their region. The missionaries then moved on to continue their work elsewhere. Always they expected the local group of Christians to maintain a clear and productive witness.

MAKING THE TRUTH PERSONAL

1 / Who is involved in your chapter, and in what ways?_____

_____

_____

_____

_____

2 / What is your group doing through personal contact to prepare non-Christians to understand an evangelistic speaker?_____

_____

_____

_____

3 / List any specific steps your group can take to strengthen its witness.____

_____

_____

PERSONAL REACTIONS / questions, commitments, prayer requests

SUGGESTIONS FOR FURTHER STUDY
TEXTS / Acts 2:43-47; 18:24-28; Ephesians 3:10
LITERATURE / "A Forum on Campus Impact," HIS, Dec. 1973
Don Smith, "Group Witness," HIS, Mar. 1972

SCRIPTURE READING / Matthew 28:18–20; II Corinthians 5:16–20; Ezekiel 33:7–10

1 / When do I become responsible for reaching others for Christ?_____

_____

2 / Have I accepted this as simultaneously a great privilege and heavy responsibility?_____

SUMMARY OF TEACHING

Every Christian is a missionary. This is clearly taught in the Word of God. Our Lord gave the Great Commission which involves us all. Paul echoes this when he points out that we are ambassadors for Christ: God makes His appeal through us; we stand in the place of Christ! Has the realization that you are Christ's representative to your roommate, lab partner, parents, friends ever fully gripped you?

God is doing a mighty work in history of calling out for Himself a people "from every tribe and tongue and people and nation." He is building His Church and one day will bring it to completion. Nothing will thwart His purpose (see Matthew 16:18). The amazing thing is that God allows us to participate in His work as instruments in His hand. God could have commissioned angels to evangelize, but He has chosen us. God seeks men through men. He has no feet but our feet, no mouth but our mouths, no hands but our hands. We are workers together with Him (II Corinthians 6:1).

Privilege always brings responsibility, however. Paul in Acts 20:26 told the Ephesian elders he was free from the blood of all of them. Evidently he was referring to the solemn warning given in Ezekiel 33:7–10. The full meaning of this is not clear, but the implication is that we shall be held accountable if we fail in our responsibility as "watchmen" to warn people of the judgment to come and to tell them of the good news of the love of God in Christ.

In evangelism, as in salvation, we are confronted with the mysterious interplay of divine sovereignty and human responsibility. God is doing a work, but He uses us as instruments. Someone has said that the Holy Spirit does not present the gospel. This work He has left exclusively to us. But we can never convert anyone. Only the Holy Spirit can do that. As we understand

49

God's part and our part in evangelism, we are delivered from the twin mistakes of pride and despair. There is no cause for pride if God chooses to use us as the last link in the chain of events leading to a person's conversion. Neither is there ground for despair because we feel unable to convince a blinded mind or produce response from a rebellious will.

Thus prayer is absolutely vital to effective evangelism: that God the Holy Spirit will work and that we will be enabled to be used by Him. Being willing to be used in the answer to our prayer is also essential.

When the term evangelism is used, we usually think of mass meetings. But even Billy Graham points out that mass evangelism is only effective as it becomes personal in the counseling of individuals after the mass meeting. On campus there is a definite place for large meetings and extensive evangelism: i.e., presenting the message to a group wider than the circle of friends the Christians have. All-campus lectures, informal discussions in fraternities, sororities, and dormitories, films and other activities are useful in presenting the message widely. These activities, however, are usually successful only as each Christian is an effective personal evangelist.

Our primary responsibility in evangelism is to the people we see repeatedly rather than to the stranger whom we may see once but never again.

But many students don't know how to witness personally though they recognize their privilege and responsibility in evangelism. This week we will study the motivation in evangelism, possible attitudes toward non-Christians, how to introduce spiritual matters into conversation, the place of reason, how to help a person come to a decision, and the importance of follow-up of those who have come to know Christ. It will not be an academic study, but one that will involve us with people.

MAKING THE TRUTH PERSONAL

1 / List the people on the campus for whom you think God has given you primary responsibility as an ambassador and watchman._____

_____

2 / How may the awareness that God is building His Church give you confidence to launch out in witness?_____

PERSONAL REACTIONS / questions, commitments, prayer requests

SUGGESTIONS FOR FURTHER STUDY
TEXT / Acts 4
LITERATURE / John R. W. Stott, *Personal Evangelism* (IVP, 1964)
Paul Little, *How to Give Away Your Faith* (IVP, 1966)
Note: the place of prayer in evangelism is not covered at length this week. But see Unit 1, Day 7 in this guide.

PURPOSE / To show the necessary motivation toward God and man for effective evangelism.

SCRIPTURE READING / I Corinthians 13; II Corinthians 5:11–21

1 / What is the relationship between your witness and your love for God and people?_____

_____

2 / Why is love more important than anything else in Christian experience?

_____

SUMMARY OF TEACHING

A new Christian usually witnesses very effectively with few inhibitions. Why? Because he has had an experience that is real and he wants to share a good thing with everyone else. These two elements, reality and conviction, are basic to any effective witness.

How do we come to this reality and conviction if we don't have it? First, we must ask why we do not have it. On analysis it usually becomes clear that a sense of unreality in the life of a genuine Christian stems either from an area of rebellion and holdout against the will of God or some unconfessed sin. These conditions cause the Christian life to become a burden. Non-Christians who know people like this tend to view Christianity as vapid, tasteless, and the kind of thing that is best avoided.

If our relationship to Christ is a "have to" rather than a "want to" relationship, we will never witness effectively. To attempt to witness under those conditions is to attempt an odious chore and to offer something that is unattractive.

Our Lord said that it was "out of the abundance of the heart" that the mouth speaks. Unless we have a genuine, vital, day-by-day relationship with Him, there is no experience from which to speak with conviction. Total commitment to the will of God and a day-by-day fellowship with Him in prayer and meditation in the Word of God are fundamental prerequisites to a living experience that overflows to others. Having experienced the greatest thing in all of life through Jesus Christ, we want to share Him with others.

Not only do we need a love for the Lord Jesus Christ which makes us want to please Him by bearing testimony to His life and work for us, but we must love people as well. If we view them simply as abstract souls to be saved, apart from their total personality, they will react against us as not being really interested in them and we will be denying the nature of our message which is love. As a result, our desire to win them to Christ will be defeated. I Corinthians 13 spells out in very concrete terms the meaning of the abstract idea of love. Love alone overcomes barriers of hostility and indifference. The absence of love is fatal no matter what other qualities or how much zeal we may have.

Love for God and love for man are basic if we are to be effective ambassadors for Jesus Christ.

MAKING THE TRUTH PERSONAL

1 / Do you earnestly desire to share Jesus Christ with others?_____

If not, why not?_____

_____

2 / Meditate on the love of Christ to you. What response does this bring

in your own heart?_____

_____

_____

"Love so amazing, so divine, Demands my soul, my life, my all."

PERSONAL REACTIONS / questions, commitments, prayer requests

SUGGESTIONS FOR FURTHER STUDY
TEXTS / Mark 6:30-34; 1 Thessalonians 2:7, 8
LITERATURE / J. I. Packer, *Evangelism and the Sovereignty of God* (IVP, 1961)
Paul Little, "Before You Pass It On," HIS, Feb. 1972.

PURPOSE / To learn principles of contact with non-Christians.

SCRIPTURE READING / Luke 5:27–32; 7:31–50

1 / Why is it necessary for us to spend time with non-Christians?_____

_____

2 / What was our Lord's instruction and example in His relationships with

non-Christians?_____

_____

SUMMARY OF TEACHING

Our Lord promises to make us fishers of men as we follow Him. By this figure of speech He implies that in order to catch fish, we must go where fish are. If we are to witness to non-Christians, we must make ourselves available for natural contact with them. Our Lord was an example of this. He was accused by His Pharisee friends of being a friend of publicans and sinners—an accusation He did not deny.

Many Christians blunder by equating separation from the world with isolation from the world (John 17:15). This tragic misunderstanding effectively prevents the spread of the gospel. If you knew a number of people who had scarlet fever and you wanted to prevent the disease from spreading, what would you do? The answer is simple. Put everyone who has scarlet fever together. In a hospital this is called the isolation ward. What more effective way to keep the gospel from spreading can be found than to convince Christians that they should spend all of their time with each other and have nothing to do, except for necessary, temporary contacts, with those who do not know the Savior.

But if we are to live in the world yet not be of it, we must face certain problems. We live in a world whose social standards tend to differ from those of the Christian community. How can we penetrate this society to witness without at the same time succumbing to compromise?

First, we must learn not to communicate an attitude of condemnation to non-Christians for their so-called worldly behavior. They are only doing what to them is natural. If they feel condemned in our presence, they will avoid us, and we will have lost the opportunity to share the gospel with them. We are not condoning a person's behavior if we fail to condemn it. Our Lord did not condone the behavior of the woman taken in adultery whose story is in John 8, but he said, "Neither do I condemn thee: go, and sin no more."

Second, we must anticipate those social situations which could cause embarrassment because of conflicting social standards. By giving prior thought as to how we will respond, we can usually eliminate embarrassment and tension that results from awkward, hesitant behavior.

For instance: Your roommate or lab partner invites you to have a drink or participate in some other activity that as a Christian you want to avoid. If you say, "No thanks, I don't drink. I'm a Christian," two things happen. Your friend feels condemned as a pagan and he gains the impression that not drinking (or whatever it is he has suggested) is a basic part of Christianity. This—of course—is not the case. Thousands of non-Christians do not drink, etc., but in some cultures, some Christians do. The solution is to substitute another activity which will preserve the friendship. You can say without apology, "No thanks. Personally, I don't care for beer, but let's go out and have a coke." In this way you accept the compliment that you have been paid by being invited to spend time with your friend and substitute on the spot something you can both do. This principle of substitution has application in a variety of situations.

In developing friendship and a liking for a non-Christian we need to become interested in the wholesome things that appeal to him though we may not have been attracted to these before.

MAKING THE TRUTH PERSONAL

1 / Have I condemned non-Christians unwittingly in the last week?_____

How?_____

_____

2 / Am I isolated from non-Christians so that not even one would think of me as a friend to whom they would turn in a time of need? _____

How?_____

_____

_____

Why?_____

What can I do to change this?_____

3 / What social conflicts make me uneasy in the presence of non-Christians?

_____

_____

How can I overcome this the next time?_____

_____

PERSONAL REACTIONS / questions, commitments, prayer requests

SUGGESTIONS FOR FURTHER STUDY
LITERATURE / Paul Little, *Lost Audience* (IVP, 1959)
HIS, Mar. 1974; Mar. 1976 (the whole issue)

PURPOSE / To suggest ways of turning conversation to spiritual matters.

SCRIPTURE READING / John 4:1–26

1 / How did Jesus take the initiative with the Samaritan woman?_____

_____

2 / Trace the progression of the woman's curiosity. How did Jesus arouse

it?_____

_____

SUMMARY OF TEACHING

Effective witness to Jesus Christ depends upon a consistent life and clear verbal communication of the gospel. A false antithesis between these two is sometimes suggested by the question, "Which is more important, the life that I live or the words that I say?" This is like asking, "Which wing of an airplane is more important, the right or the left?" Of course, the answer is neither— both are absolutely essential. Life and lip are both indispensable in personal witness to Jesus Christ.

If I am a hypocrite, it is better that I say nothing about the Lord. On the other hand, though my life be exemplary, if I do not bear witness to the Source of that life I rob God of His glory and others of knowing how they may receive this life for themselves.

Many Christians are stymied because they do not know how to introduce the gospel into conversation. We must pray each day that God the Holy Spirit will lead us to those who are open. He often does as we take initiative in throwing out leading questions in a conversation. This device enables us to discover any interest that God has already aroused, evidenced by the person's response to these questions. We cannot create openness; only the Holy Spirit can do this, but He will help us to uncover spiritual hunger that He has created.

Our Lord in His conversation with the woman at the well first established common ground with her by talking about water. We must begin by talking with people about the things that interest them, if we want them eventually to talk about things that stimulate us. The following series of questions asked after a period of casual conversation has proven to be very helpful to many Christians in launching a conversation about the gospel.

1. Are you interested in spiritual things? The response to this is either yes or no.

2. What would you say a real Christian is? Most people respond by saying, "Someone who goes to church," "Someone who lives a good life," etc. This then gives you a chance to define the term adequately.

3. Would you like to become a real Christian now?

The value of these questions is that we know in advance where we are going in the conversation. This relieves us of nervousness and enables us to talk in the same casual, quiet, confident manner and tone of voice in which we have been discussing everything else.

Another way to take initiative in conversation is in turning to personal experience. As we get well acquainted with non-Christians, they will begin to share with us their fears, frustrations, anxieties and problems. When they do, we can say, "You know, I used to feel that way until I had an experience that completely changed my life. Would you like me to tell you about it?" We indicate to the person that we know how they feel and that we have found the solution to the problem. However, we do not force ourselves on them but allow them to invite us to tell how we came to solve those problems. If we have been raised in a Christian home and have not had a dramatic experience, or perhaps one that does not exactly parallel what the person mentions, we can say, "I would feel that way if it weren't for an experience that completely changed my life." As you think and pray about it, other possibilities of taking initiative will come to mind.

People who have been used of God in personal evangelism have had a sense of expectancy, an alertness to discover spiritual interest. They have also taken the initiative to uncover that interest. If no response is evident, they drop the subject and continue the conversation about more impersonal matters. By being able to move in or move on to something else as the circumstances warrant, we are relieved of the pressure and frustration that comes from feeling we have to force the gospel on people who resent the overture. There are so many people all around us who are hungry for spiritual reality that we do not have to waste time and energy forcing ourselves on those who are not.

MAKING THE TRUTH PERSONAL

1 / List three people whom you will ask the above questions before the next cell meeting.

2 / Pray that God will give an open and interested response to these questions.

3 / Be prepared to share your experience at the next cell meeting as others tell how they, too, took initiative in conversation.

SUGGESTIONS FOR FURTHER STUDY
TEXTS / Isaiah 50:4; Exodus 4:10-12
LITERATURE / Paul Little, "Plan for Stalled Conversations," HIS, Mar. 1973.
Bill Tiffan, "Meet Them Where They Are," HIS, Mar. 1973.
K. F. W. Prior, *The Gospel in a Pagan Society* (IVP, 1975)

PURPOSE / To see the place of reason in personal witness

SCRIPTURE READING / I Corinthians 1:18–2:15; Acts 17:16–34, I Peter 3:15

1 / Why is it impossible for a non-Christian to "see" the truth of the gospel?

2 / With whom do we battle in prayer for the souls of men?_____

SUMMARY OF TEACHING

The Scripture clearly teaches that the natural man cannot understand spiritual things apart from the enlightenment of the Holy Spirit. At the same time, Christians are commanded to be able to give a reason for the hope that is within them. This seeming contradiction is explained when we realize that a reasonable presentation of the gospel is often an instrument that the Holy Spirit uses to enlighten natural men. The realization of this relationship enables us to avoid two extremes. The first is a tendency to adopt an anti-intellectual attitude which scorns any reasoned presentation of the gospel as useless and possibly even harmful. It suggests that the "simple gospel" is all that is necessary. This point of view is disastrous to Christian and non-Christian alike. The Christian, because he never really faces up to basic intellectual issues, begins eventually to wonder if there are answers to the questions he is being constantly asked and which come up in his own mind despite his attempts to suppress them. The non-Christian, thinking that there are no answers to his honest questions and wishing to maintain his intellectual integrity, turns a deaf ear to what he thinks is essentially naive nonsense. John Stott has said, "We cannot pander to a man's intellectual arrogance, but we must cater to his intellectual integrity."

The other extreme is to suppose that by carefully reasoned argument and human logic we can persuade someone to become a Christian. Reason never caused a proud rebellious will to submit to the authority of the Lord Jesus Christ. Only the Holy Spirit can do this. Ultimately, the issue in becoming a Christian is moral rather than intellectual. But for his own confidence as well as for the benefit of honest seekers, the Christian needs to have answers to the questions he is frequently asked. This is not so awesome a task as one might think at first. Careful reflection will bring to light the fact that there are only a few basic questions that non-Christians tend to ask. By getting the answers to these questions through study and conversation with more experienced

Christians, one increases his own confidence in the truth of the gospel and is able to help the non-Christian to consider evidence of which he is usually unaware.

MAKING THE TRUTH PERSONAL

1 / List the three questions you are most afraid of being asked by non-Christians._____

_____

2 / Determine the specific steps you are going to take to get answers to them.

_____

3 / Thank God that your eyes have been opened to see the Truth.

PERSONAL REACTIONS / questions, commitments, prayer requests

SUGGESTIONS FOR FURTHER STUDY
TEXT / Acts 26
LITERATURE / Paul Little, *Know Why You Believe* (IVP, 1968)
Oliver Barclay, *Reasons for Faith* (IVP, 1974)
J. N. D. Anderson, *Evidence for the Resurrection* (IVP, 1966)
Kenneth Taylor, *Is Christianity Credible?* (IVP, 1951)

PURPOSE / To discover how to invite a person to receive Jesus Christ.

SCRIPTURE ILLUSTRATION / Matthew 16:13–15; 19:16–22; Acts 17:22, 32–34

1 / Why is a decision about Jesus Christ so urgent?_____

_____

2 / What may happen when a person decides to "postpone" a decision?

_____

SUMMARY OF TEACHING

Fishing without a hook is not very productive. But we do it with alarming frequency in personal evangelism. Every time we fail to invite a person to receive Jesus Christ we are fishers for men without a hook.

It is worse than useless, however, to pressure a person into a decision. We can get people to agree with us easily, but if this agreement and "decision" is not the work of the Holy Spirit serious harm has been done. The person will likely be harder than ever to reach and what is even worse may be falsely assured that he is a Christian.

On the other hand, there are many many people who long for spiritual reality. They are just waiting to be asked and want to have explained to them how to take the step. Still others need to realize that a personal decision about Jesus Christ is not something optional but a matter of life and death significance. They need to realize that to postpone a decision is to have made a decision against Jesus Christ.

After conversation about spiritual things, following a Bible study or church service, or after an evangelistic discussion, the following series of questions have helped many students come to the point of decision without offense.

1. Have you ever trusted Christ or are you still on the way? Sometimes a person will say, "What do you mean by personally trusting Christ?" This is a clue that he is probably not a Christian and gives you the opening to explain what it is to be born again as well as to invite him to take that step. Usually he will say, "I'm still on the way."

2. How far along the way are you? Here a person describes to us exactly where he is in his thinking. From this we may discover that he is not ready to make a decision. On the other hand, we may find that he believes all the facts about the Lord Jesus Christ but does not know how to take the final step of receiving Him into his life.

3. Would you like to become a Christian now? When we invite a person to become a Christian, we need to warn them against two dangers. The first is precipitous action through which they might rush into a decision without having first counted the cost. The tremendous implications of becoming a Christian should be realized before a commitment is made. On the other hand, procrastination must be avoided. When a person has understood how to become a Christian and the implications of this step, it is a very dangerous thing to put this decision off. No one has the guarantee of seeing tomorrow morning's sunrise, and this is the most urgent and far-reaching decision that any person ever makes in his whole life.

MAKING THE TRUTH PERSONAL

1 / Write down the name of someone whom you believe may be ready to

become a Christian._____

2 / Pray that the Holy Spirit will enable you to invite him to take this step very soon and that he will be open to it.

PERSONAL REACTIONS / questions, commitments, prayer requests

SUGGESTIONS FOR FURTHER STUDY
LITERATURE / Michael Green, *The Brink of Decision* (IVP, 1964)
John R. W. Stott, *Becoming a Christian* (IVP, 1950)

PURPOSE / To understand areas in which new Christians most frequently need help.

SCRIPTURE READING / II Timothy 2:1, 2; I Peter 2:2, 3; I John 5:11–15

1 / What is the ultimate objective of follow-up?_____

_____

2 / What constitutes spiritual food for the Christian?_____

_____

SUMMARY OF TEACHING

When a person first becomes a Christian, he is a spiritual baby. Just as physical babies need someone to help them, spiritual babies need help too. If we have been used of God to introduce a person to the Lord Jesus Christ, it is our primary responsibility to follow them up and help them come to maturity in Christ.

The Apostle Paul is an excellent example of one who followed up those to whom he had been a spiritual blessing. His letters reveal the deep love he had for his spiritual children. He prayed for them regularly and sent them spiritual counsel and instruction by letter when he was not able to talk to them in person.

Most new Christians need special help in several areas.

1. They need to be able to understand the big picture of what God has been doing in history in building His Church. This will help them to fit their own experience into the overall pattern of God's work. This involves a complete understanding of the gospel as well as a panoramic view of God's work in building the Church.

2. A new Christian needs to know immediately how to take in spiritual food by reading and meditating in the Scripture. He needs to learn something of communion in prayer with the living God. The booklet, *Quiet Time* is extremely valuable here, and he should be encouraged to begin a daily systematic reading of the Scripture. *Light on the Way* is highly recommended as a systematic Bible reading for one month. It

combines the advantages of a brief comment and a provocative question along with a memory verse and a suggestion for prayer arising out of the passage. It then leads into a six-month study course followed by a three-year course that takes the student through the whole Bible.

3. Assurance of salvation is often a problem. New Christians tend to depend on their feelings as a barometer of their certainty of salvation. They need to be shown that our certainty comes from faith in the Lord Jesus Christ and what He has done for us. We have accepted Him at His word. Feelings, by their very nature, vary and are not a sure guide of anything. The new Christian should be encouraged to memorize I John 5:11, 12.

4. The problem of sin. Many new Christians are tempted by Satan to think that they cannot possibly be saved because sin is still in their lives. Others have erroneously been led to believe that having become Christians, they would no longer find sin to be a problem. Instead they find it to be a greater problem than ever before. It is important that they see that our relationship with the Lord Jesus Christ is established once and for all when, through faith and trust in Him, we are born into the family of God. Sin mars our communion and fellowship with God but does not basically alter or destroy our relationship to Him as children. A little boy who disobeys his father does not cease to be a son, but his communication and friendship with his father is strained until there is confession and restoration. So it is in the Christian life.

Sin does not cease to be a problem in the Christian life, but our attitude toward sin changes. A Christian cannot possibly adopt the attitude that since he has been forgiven he can live as he pleases. This is clearcut evidence that a person has never really been born again. When one becomes a new creature in Christ, his whole outlook changes. His desire now is to please the Lord Jesus Christ. Sin becomes abhorrent to him, and though he may fall into it, he will not willfully, joyfully, zestfully persist in it. I John 1:9 is another verse a new Christian should memorize very early in his Christian experience.

5. A new Christian needs help in thinking through his relationships as a Christian. Often he unwisely breaks all connections with his non-Christian friends at the very moment when he has the greatest opportunity to witness to them. They are able to see the change in his life, but if he cuts himself off from them, they have no opportunity to discover from him the source of his life. On the other hand, if his acquaintances drag him back into temptation and evil, he may have to break off with them completely.

Parental relationships must be thought through also. Lack of consideration and love in the way one tells one's parents he has become a Christian can close the door for witness for many years to come. In talking or writing to parents it is best to assume that they know the facts of the gospel. The new Christian can relate how these facts have just become meaningful to him by describing his Christian experience. This may draw out questions from the parents and pave the way for further conversation. Sometimes parents have been informed in a spirit of condemnation that their child has become a Christian. This has caused deep hurt and sometimes bitterness. An older Christian can help a young Christian avoid a great many mistakes by discussing with him and praying with him about his relationships.

It is essential that wherever possible a new Christian meet once a week with an older Christian for prayer, Bible study, and a time of sharing. This gives the new Christian opportunity to ask any questions that may have come up in his mind in the previous week. It is best to have a systematic plan of study which can be deviated from as other questions arise. The Bible study booklet, *Christ in You,* is very helpful for a week by week follow up study you can do together. It covers in a Christ-centered way a number of the areas described above.

MAKING THE TRUTH PERSONAL

1 / Write down the name of at least one person with whom you could begin

to meet on a weekly basis for prayer and Bible study._____

2 / Take steps to assemble the materials that would enable you to systematically follow up a new Christian._____

_____

3 / Pray that you will have a new Christian to follow up very soon.

PERSONAL REACTIONS / questions, commitments, prayer requests

SUGGESTIONS FOR FURTHER STUDY
LITERATURE / Michael Griffiths, *Encouraging New Christians* (IVP, 1964)
Quiet Time (IVP, 1976)
Christ in You (IVP, 1956)

SECTION II / Living Out the Christian Life

SCRIPTURE READING / John 10:1–16

It is perplexing to know that the Christian life must involve self-denial and fulfillment, struggle and peace, hardship and abundance, sorrows and joy. In part, these tensions result from our dual citizenship; we are members of the kingdom of God, yet are citizens of this world.

Since we want to give whole-hearted allegiance to God, we must consider our relationship to the world. Are we just marking time until God rescues us out of this hopelessly evil world? Does it make any difference how we live now, since our salvation is assured by God and will be completed at Christ's coming? Are we neglecting the legitimate enjoyment of people and things through misunderstanding? Should we withdraw from all non-Christian relationships in order not to be of the world? Is there a standard by which we can accurately judge our conduct so we can tell where it should differ from other people's?

This week we will look at some aspects of our relationship to God, the world, and the things and people in it, in hope of answering various questions about right attitudes and behavior.

ASSIGNMENT

1 / For the next two days evaluate yourself and make a list of what you consider worldly acts and behavior. Draw these items from what you do or are tempted to do during this time, and try to be as inclusive as possible.

2 / After you have made your list, analyze the recurrent attitudes that lie at the base of your view of worldliness. Then write a two-to-five-sentence definition of worldliness as you understand it. Have you left out any aspect?

5 / Wholesome
Participation in Life

SET APART TO GOD
IN THE WORLD / DAY 2

PURPOSE / To see that we do not belong to ourselves but to God, and that what we are and do must be for His sake.

SCRIPTURE READING / Titus 2:11–14; Ephesians 5:25–27; II Timothy 2:20–23

1 / How did Jesus Christ's death for us change our *condition* and *goals?*

(Titus and Ephesians) _____

_____

_____

_____

2 / What positive and negative actions are to result in the Christian's life? Why? (II Timothy) _____

_____

_____

SUMMARY OF TEACHING

Before we knew God we were slaves of Satan, sin, and death. Because He loved us and bought us back, we are now God's exclusive possession. We have been singled out to know, love, and serve Him. These facts are basic if we are to appreciate and enjoy life. The Old Testament picture of a bondslave is an appropriate analogy to our position: we are men who bear the marks of our Master publicly as a proof of His ownership and our love. We are distinct from other men.

Jesus Christ chose us for Himself and gave Himself for us in death, so that we could be cleansed from our sin and made pure. Eventually all His chosen ones are to be presented to Him as a bride without flaw. Being set apart to God is therefore a group relationship as well as an individual calling. And what we are affects others.

We are not passive spectators in this matter. God calls on us to cleanse

70

ourselves from what is defiling so that we will be usable for His purposes. Having been made new in Jesus Christ, we must adopt God's view of the world and act in accordance with it.

MAKING THE TRUTH PERSONAL

1 / How will your actions toward other people today show that you belong to God? (Give two or three specifics.)_____

_____

_____

2 / Why are you likely to have conflicts if you are serious about showing your allegiance to Jesus Christ? What kind of conflicts will they be?_____

_____

_____

_____

_____

PERSONAL REACTIONS / questions, commitments, prayer requests

SUGGESTIONS FOR FURTHER STUDY
TEXTS / Exodus 21:1-6; 1 Corinthians 6:9-11; 1 Peter 1:2
LITERATURE / Michael Green, *New Life, New Lifestyle* (IVP, 1973)

5 / Wholesome Participation in Life

PURPOSE / To see the change in our character that is to result when we are made sons of God.

SCRIPTURE READING / I Peter 1:13–22; Romans 8:12–17, 28, 29

1 / Give three reasons why holiness must not be neglected by the believer.

(I Peter)_____

_____

_____

_____

2 / What does God's purpose for the believer (Romans 8:29) tell you about

the kind of character he is to have?_____

_____

How do vss. 12–14 explain this?_____

_____

SUMMARY OF TEACHING

God made man in His image, but man's likeness to God's moral character has been violently altered because of sin. Having restored us to the legal status of sonship by the death of Christ, God desires to complete His work in us by making our conduct holy. From before the foundation of the world He has planned that we should become like Jesus Christ in character, thus making us completely new men. Today He is working in everything toward that good end.

We must cooperate with Him by turning from sin and obeying the Holy Spirit who teaches us what is right. Holiness, or conformity to Jesus Christ is not achieved instantly. It is a process of alteration, excision, and growth, in which our minds, affections, and wills are renewed so that our behavior increasingly reflects the life of our Lord. Becoming like Jesus Christ will result in our highest good and God's glory.

MAKING THE TRUTH PERSONAL

1 / Why should God's work of holiness in your life make you a more attractive and pleasant person to know?_____

_____

_____

_____ Are you?_____

2 / How will cooperation with God in this work affect your participation in life on campus?_____

_____

_____

_____

PERSONAL REACTIONS / questions, commitments, prayer requests

SUGGESTIONS FOR FURTHER STUDY
TEXTS / 2 Peter 3:8-14; Ephesians 1:3-6; 1 Thessalonians 4:3-8
LITERATURE / J. I. Packer, *Knowing God* (IVP, 1973), pp. 181-208.

5 / Wholesome
Participation in Life

PURPOSE / To see how God wants the Christian to regard the world of things
He has made.

SCRIPTURE READING / I Timothy 4:1–5, 6:17

1 / What is wrong in condemning the use and enjoyment of material goods?

_____

_____

_____

2 / How does God want you to regard (positively and negatively) the world
of things?_____

_____

_____

SUMMARY OF TEACHING

When God created the world He declared that it was good. He approved all
its parts because they fitted into His scheme; He had created a good order of
things out of chaos.

Man has sinned, and by consequence all creation has become subject to
decay and death. Because God has redeemed us from bondage to death and
given us spiritual life, some Christians look on the material world as evil and to
be shunned. They consider association with some parts of this world of things
as an unfortunate necessity for physical existence. In their eyes, it is "worldly"
to enjoy good food, nice clothing, comfortable homes. But we must affirm
that God is the Author of all things and that He has given them to us to use
and enjoy. We honor Him when we receive His gifts thankfully and use them
in the right way.

We must understand God's intention for His creation if we are to use His
gifts properly. (Any movement away from His plan is toward chaos again.)
We misuse His gifts chiefly by not thanking Him for them and by making them
ends in life. It is possible to become so thing-centered that we put the attain-

74

ment and enjoyment of material pleasures before loving and obeying God. That is idolatry. Overindulgence, grasping for more than we need, refusal to share what we have, using good to other people's harm, and placing our confidence in our wealth (however small): these are sin. As we take pleasure in God's gifts with thankfulness and in obedience to His commands, we glorify Him and proclaim Him Lord of creation.

MAKING THE TRUTH PERSONAL

1 / How can wrong understanding of God's attitude toward the world of created things cause you to confuse the meaning of worldliness?_____

_____

_____

_____

2 / What attitudes are necessary for you to use things in a way pleasing to God?_____

_____

_____

_____

PERSONAL REACTIONS / questions, commitments, prayer requests

SUGGESTIONS FOR FURTHER STUDY
TEXTS / Matthew 6:25-33; Romans 1:18-25; 14:13-23
LITERATURE / Michael Griffiths, *Unsplitting Your Christian Life* (IVP, 1973), pp. 81-93.

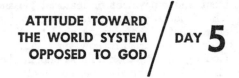
PURPOSE / To see what "the world" is, of which the Christian is not to be a part.

SCRIPTURE READING / John 15:18–22; James 3:13–4:5; I John 2:15–17

1 / How does the apostle James contrast spiritual and worldly wisdom as to their source and outworking?_____

_____

_____

_____

2 / According to John what are the motivating principles of "the world"?
_____Why does
the world hate the Christian?_____

_____

SUMMARY OF TEACHING

The word *world* is used with several meanings in Scripture: all created things, all people, the present age, a world order, and all the people who are opposed to God. The world of which the Christian is not to be a part is that system or spirit opposed to God, who is truth and righteousness. Our subjection to this spirit expresses itself in three forms: the lust of the flesh, the lust of the eyes, and the pride of life. (See I John 2:16, NEB. "Everything the world affords, all that panders to the appetites, or entices the eyes, all the glamour of its life, springs not from the Father but from the godless world.") Worldliness is the attitude of using God's gifts without reference to Him: for self-indulgence and without thankfulness.

The Christian lives in the midst of a world system that is opposed to God, but is rescued out of it, and must refuse to have anything to do with it. The world always appeals to the Christian to conform to its pattern of self-indulgence. But he must oppose this, and by godly living, bear witness to the truth as a light in a dark place.

Some Christians think that worldliness means to take part in certain social practices. Such a definition is a limited concept of worldliness and often misses the heart of the matter: worldliness is self-indulgence in any area of life. A divided heart says "I love and obey God," yet seeks its own satisfaction. The Bible calls this spiritual adultery, for the Christian must give his heart, mind, and body to God, and not to another—not even himself.

The world will hate the true Christian for the same reason it hated Jesus Christ. By refusing to conform to it and by living a holy life, the Christian exposes the world's essential self-centeredness and thus arouses its hatred.

MAKING THE TRUTH PERSONAL

1 / In light of the three expressions that worldliness can take, how can the Christian conform to the world in the following practices: praying aloud or giving a testimony, choosing someone for a date, buying and wearing clothes?

_____

_____

_____

_____

2 / Why, even when we're aware of them, do we sometimes not want to give up our worldly attitudes?_____

_____

_____

PERSONAL REACTIONS / questions, commitments, prayer requests

SUGGESTIONS FOR FURTHER STUDY
TEXTS / Colossians 3:1-17; John 16:33
LITERATURE / Michael Griffiths, *Unsplitting Your Christian Life* (IVP, 1973)
Francis A. Schaeffer, *The God Who Is There* (IVP, 1968), pp. 13-84.

PURPOSE / To see what a godly attitude toward people is, in a world opposed to God.

SCRIPTURE READING / John 17:13–23; I Corinthians 9:19–23

1 / According to Jesus, what was to be the relationship of His disciples to the world?_____

_____

_____

2 / What motives are to be active in the Christian's relationship to people? (I Corinthians)_____

_____

_____

SUMMARY OF TEACHING

Our Lord has sent us into the world to bear witness so that the world can know who He is and believe in Him. We are to be lights in their sight.

As recipients of God's grace, Christians have a debt to discharge by bringing the gospel to those who have not heard it. We must no longer look at ourselves or others from a human point of view, but see people as God does: sinners in need of grace before judgment comes. This will cause us to see the urgency of proclaiming God's love and provision for forgiveness and life.

In order to communicate the truth we will have to be identified with people, but not with their sins. Jesus gives us the example to follow. He was a friend of publicans and sinners and yet was without sin Himself. We can neither withdraw from society nor capitulate to the world in its view and practice of life. While reaching out to the sinner with compassion and understanding, we are to abhor the sin and stand in fear and humility lest we also fall.

MAKING THE TRUTH PERSONAL

1 / List three ways in which you can become more closely identified with the

students on your campus for the sake of the gospel without sharing in their sins._____

_____

_____

_____

2 / Why should the Christian be free from regarding non-Christians as threats to his security, means of improving his social status, or annoyances to be avoided?_____

_____

_____How should he regard them?_____

_____

PERSONAL REACTIONS / questions, commitments, prayer requests

SUGGESTIONS FOR FURTHER STUDY
TEXTS / 1 Corinthians 5:9-11; 2 Corinthians 5:11-20; Jude 17-23
LITERATURE / Paul Little, *Lost Audience* (IVP, 1959)
Francis A. Schaeffer, *The Mark of the Christian* (IVP, 1970)

5 / Wholesome Participation in Life

PURPOSE / To see how God wants us to regard our work.

SCRIPTURE READING / Colossians 3:22–4:1; I Thessalonians 4:10–12; Acts 20:33–35

1 / Why can a Christian work heartily at a secular job? (Colossians)_____

_____

_____

2 / What should be the results of our work? (I Thessalonians and Acts)

_____

_____

SUMMARY OF TEACHING

From the beginning of man's history, even before the Fall, work has been the normal activity of life. After the entry of sin, God ordained that man should earn his living by the sweat of his brow. This was a good adjustment for man because of the change in his moral condition and the change in nature due to the curse (see Genesis 3).

Each man is to work heartily, giving himself with vigor to his responsibilities. For the Christian there is greater motivation than just knowing that he must work in order to live: even when his employers are godless men he serves the Lord Jesus by his work. God intends His children to be able to enjoy their work and do it gladly. If called to work in a secular job, the Christian need not feel he is serving the Lord less acceptably than the man employed in some kind of church work. God appoints them both and is pleased by their faithfulness in doing what He has entrusted to them.

The Christian must work to provide for the needs of his family, and also in order to help others in need. His industry should command the respect of outsiders and keep him from being a burden on anyone. He knows that all must share in work, and that those who don't work when they can don't deserve to eat. As he works he must respect his employer since the Lord has called him to serve that man.

MAKING THE TRUTH PERSONAL

1 / What Christian principles of work seem particularly at odds with current attitudes?_____

_____

_____

2 / How can you serve Jesus Christ in writing class papers, taking tests, and participating in quiz sections?_____

_____

_____Does your output show that He's a worthy object of your best efforts?_____

_____

PERSONAL REACTIONS / questions, commitments, prayer requests

SUGGESTIONS FOR FURTHER STUDY
TEXTS / Genesis 3:17-19; Ephesians 4:28; 2 Thessalonians 3:6-12
LITERATURE / John White, *The Fight* (IVP, 1976), pp. 201-14.

SCRIPTURE READING / Mark 7:14–23

Much contemporary literature shows man as anxiety-ridden, with a sense of futility and lack of purpose, insulated against others, alienated from himself, groping for clues to life's meaning, and yearning for fulfillment. He cannot cope with an increasingly complex and impersonal society, and he numbly contemplates the possibility that the world's grand climax will be nuclear annihilation. Despite his cleverness, all he does seems to turn to ashes at his touch, and the old world of optimistic anticipation seems gone forever.

Not everyone sees life in this way, of course, but a significant number of authors and artists have disclosed the sickness of our time. The symptoms of man's predicament indicate his basic disease, sin. It isn't so much that external forces are thwarting his good intentions; something is wrong at the heart of man, that affects his thoughts, words, and deeds, and keeps life from being what he senses it should be.

Is the gospel relevant in this setting? The work of God in Jesus Christ provides the answer that man needs. By it He removes our guilt, provides forgiveness, implants in us a positive life-principle of goodness and meaning, restores fruitfulness, and reconciles us to Himself and to our fellow men. Our response to such overwhelming generosity and goodness must be the total dedication of our lives to God. But having experienced this introduction into a new life does not mean that all our problems disappear. Sins continue to trouble us even though our sin has been forgiven. But God provides His means to help us overcome the continuing problem of sin. The Bible shows us the truth. The Holy Spirit makes the Scriptures plain; He strengthens us to resist sin and reminds us of God's holiness and will for us.

As we contemplate God's character and work we are moved to love Him, our faith in His working is strengthened, and we learn to exercise the discipline of obedience. This week we shall study various aspects of sin and its relation to Christian growth.

ASSIGNMENT

1 / Write a brief essay (one or two paragraphs) in which you define sin (its origin, characteristics, and consequences). Do this today.

2 / Ask three friends (preferably non-Christian) what determines whether or not an act is sinful (e.g., stealing), and whether it is always sin in every situation. Write down the gist of their answers, and evaluate them briefly from your own viewpoint.

6 / Sin and Christian Growth   WHAT IS SIN? / DAY 2

PURPOSE / To see how the Bible defines sin, and how sin is exhibited.

SCRIPTURE READING / Romans 1:18–32

1 / What is the essential nature of sin (vs. 21)?_____

_____

_____

2 / What are the results of refusing to acknowledge God?_____

_____

_____

_____

SUMMARY OF TEACHING

Sin is a continually recurrent theme in the Bible since it is the universal practice of man. It is described in many ways, but the root of all sin is a desire to live independently of God.

St. Paul described sin as our revolt against God. We know Him, but refuse to acknowledge Him or give thanks to Him. Consequently, our minds become darkened and we break all God's commands. We demonstrate our essential idolatry by counting things He has made more important than God Himself. As men fall short of God's intention for them, by their increasing and appalling degradation they show the effect of sin in the individual and society. And not only do they persist in willful scorn of God's laws, they uphold falsehood and applaud others' disobedience.

A doctrine popular today says that morality is relative to cultural standards or personal opinion. This has led to acceptance of a great number of falsehoods in the name of toleration and intellectual maturity. Despite much open denial of the truth, God's standard holds firm, and the practice of sin still results in the same blindness, idolatry, and degradation.

MAKING THE TRUTH PERSONAL

1 / Why should you be concerned if you find you're not thankful to God? (cf. I Thessalonians 5:18, Romans 5:3)_____

_____

_____

2 / How is ignorance related to sin?_____

_____

_____What does this indicate

for your study of God's Word and character?_____

_____

PERSONAL REACTIONS / questions, commitments, prayer requests

SUGGESTIONS FOR FURTHER STUDY
TEXT / Genesis 3:1-19
LITERATURE / T. C. Hammond, *In Understanding Be Men* (IVP, 1968), pp. 70-98.
John R. W. Stott, *Basic Christianity* (IVP, 1971), pp. 61-80.

PURPOSE / To see how temptations to sin come to us, and how to resist them.

SCRIPTURE READING / Hebrews 4:14–16; I Corinthians 10:11–13

1 / Why can Jesus Christ help the one who is tempted?_____

_____

_____

_____

2 / What confidence can the Christian have in the face of temptation?_____

_____

_____

SUMMARY OF TEACHING

Sin is constantly brought before the Christian by the "flesh," the devil, and the world. We must recognize these sources of temptation so that we can learn to withstand them.

The term *flesh* refers to our fallen nature. This nature tempts us to gratify our desires of mind and body in an illegitimate way, without regard to God or man. It is a keen temptation to Christians in a society of abundance where the means are available and sensual gratification is upheld as a natural right and desirable goal. The Bible tells us to flee youthful lusts, overeating, sexual promiscuity. We cannot overcome them by trying to resist through a show of strength. Nor can we conquer with ease the chief sins of the "flesh," which are pride and selfishness.

The *world* tempts us to accept its view of life by using the argument "Everyone's doing it" (griping about dining hall food, being a clothes horse). We must reject such temptation by refusing to be conformed to the world (see Unit 5 on worldliness). To withstand the pressure we must know God's Word and evaluate life by it, so that we are not duped into adopting the world's standards.

The *devil* tempts us to disbelieve the truth and ignore God's law. He tries to deceive us into accepting lies, to make us believe that he is in control rather

87

than God. The Bible tells us to submit to God and resist the devil who will then flee. Though Satan opposed Him, Jesus paid the penalty for our sin on the cross and rose from the dead. This proved that Christ is stronger than Satan and can successfully help us overcome his influence.

Jesus Christ has undergone every temptation that we can possibly encounter, and has withstood them all. Consequently, He understands our problems and can help us not to fall into sin. We are more susceptible to temptation when we are physically and spiritually run-down. By studying the Bible, praying regularly, and getting proper food and rest, we will avoid the occasion for falling due to weakness. To be tempted is not to sin, but to give in is. We should expect temptations to come, and when they do we must withstand as Scripture teaches us, by the help of the Holy Spirit, and expect to grow from the testing.

MAKING THE TRUTH PERSONAL

1 / Why is it important to understand the nature of a temptation in order to withstand it?_____

_____

_____

2 / How is your personal Bible study enabling you to meet temptation?

_____

_____

PERSONAL REACTIONS / questions, commitments, prayer requests

SUGGESTIONS FOR FURTHER STUDY
TEXTS / Matthew 4:1-11; James 1:12-15; Daniel 1
LITERATURE / John White, *The Fight* (IVP, 1976), pp. 77-96.
Hope Warwick, "Girl in a Guilty Cage," HIS, Apr. 1974.

PURPOSE / To see how God helps us when we fail and sin.

SCRIPTURE READING / I John 1:5–2:2; Hebrews 9:11–14

1 / What must we realize about ourselves and about God before we try to approach Him? (I John)_____

_____

_____

2 / How and why can we be forgiven?_____

_____

_____

_____

SUMMARY OF TEACHING

Having seen that sin must be forsaken and that help is available for withstanding temptation, what should we do if we do give in to temptation, and sin? We must confess the wrong and ask for forgiveness. That was the means by which we entered God's family, and it is the pattern for a life of continuing fellowship with Him.

Because God is holy and desires us to become like Him, we must be sensitive to sin and honest about its presence in our lives. It destroys fellowship with God and dishonors His name. This would cause us to despair if we did not know that He has provided for forgiveness as often as we need it by the death of Jesus Christ, whose blood can cleanse our heart and conscience. His tender attitude toward us was demonstrated by His willingness to forgive Peter after the disciple denied knowing the Lord (Luke 22:31, 32).

We cannot presume on the kindness and patience of God by adopting a careless attitude toward sin. True repentance is proved by turning from sin to a course of life that glorifies God through likeness to Him in character and action (good works). To maintain fellowship with God we must keep short accounts with Him by confessing and forsaking sin as soon as we recognize it.

Unless we personally grasp the meaning of God's forgiveness we will not be able to love Him, accept ourselves, or be rid of our guilt. At the heart of forgiveness is acceptance of the sinner in spite of himself. And God has already proved His willingness to accept us, in that Jesus Christ died for us while we were yet sinners.

MAKING THE TRUTH PERSONAL

1 / How have you personally sensed the results of the Lord's forgiveness?

_____

_____

_____

2 /What attitudes keep you from confessing sin as soon as you are aware

of it?_____

_____

_____

Ask God to help you be honest with Him about this and be convinced of His willingness and ability to forgive.

PERSONAL REACTIONS / questions, commitments, prayer requests

SUGGESTIONS FOR FURTHER STUDY
TEXTS / Romans 6:1-23; Luke 7:36-50; Psalm 51
LITERATURE / John R. W. Stott, *Men Made New* (IVP, 1966)

PURPOSE / To see how forgiving others affects our relationship to them and to God.

SCRIPTURE READING / Matthew 6:12–15; 18:21–35

1 / How does forgiving others affect our being forgiven by God?_____

_____

_____

2 / What enables us to see the necessity and justice of forgiving others?

_____

_____

SUMMARY OF TEACHING

The validity of our repentance to God is proved by our willingness to forgive others. In the Lord's Prayer we are taught to ask for forgiveness in the degree that we have forgiven our debtors. And unless we are willing to forgive others' sins against us, we won't be forgiven by the Father.

God's love cannot flow into hearts that are closed by hard attitudes toward others. So much does our attitude toward people affect our relationship with God that we are told to be reconciled to others before coming to worship Him. Refusal to do so is sin. Following the example of God in His patience with us, we must be willing to forgive others continually.

Confession and forgiveness among Christians open the way to true sharing of life. Because God forgives and then forgets the sin, so must we. We cannot hold grudges against others.

MAKING THE TRUTH PERSONAL

1 / What unkindnesses do you find hard to accept in other people?_____

_____

_____

_____

2 / What can you find in your behavior that might offend others? What should you do about these things?_____

_____

_____

_____

PERSONAL REACTIONS / questions, commitments, prayer requests

SUGGESTIONS FOR FURTHER STUDY
TEXTS / Luke 17:3, 4; Matthew 5:23, 24
LITERATURE / David Augsburger, *The Freedom of Forgiveness* (Moody Press, 1973)

PURPOSE / To learn the purpose of God's discipline for us and to see what our obedience proves.

SCRIPTURE READING / Hebrews 5:7–10; Hebrews 12:1–17

1 / For what reasons does God discipline us?_____

_____

_____

2 / How are we to regard His discipline?_____

_____

_____

SUMMARY OF TEACHING

The presence of sin and temptation around us makes it necessary that we fight in order to live a life pleasing to God. To aid us in our struggle against sin, God works to make us strong and mature. We have seen that He provides forgiveness for our sins as well as the sympathetic ministry of Jesus Christ who suffered the same temptations. But God does not stop there. He also provides discipline as a loving Father: correcting, punishing, teaching, testing us. He wants to cut out our practices of sin, and strengthen us to endure difficulties and resist sin and temptation (e.g., He may allow sickness to teach us patience and trust, remove friends to teach reliance on Him, bring difficult persons into our life to show us our selfishness and teach us to love).

Lest we become discouraged by the rigors of discipline we have the example of our sinless Lord who learned obedience by the things He suffered. We can also be encouraged because God's discipline is a proof of His care and our sonship. God desires our love, and equates it with obedience. To prove our love and submission to God, we (like Jesus Christ) will doubtless have to learn some lessons of obedience through suffering. But rather than complaining, we can accept such discipline with thankfulness, knowing that He acts for our good, that we may share His holiness.

MAKING THE TRUTH PERSONAL

1 / Why isn't it necessary to know specifically why some difficulty has entered your life?_____

_____

_____

2 / What kind of questions should it raise in your mind?_____

_____

_____

_____

PERSONAL REACTIONS / questions, commitments, prayer requests

SUGGESTIONS FOR FURTHER STUDY
TEXTS / John 15:9-11; 1 Samuel 26; 2 Corinthians 1:3-10; Amos 4
LITERATURE / Barbara Dill, "Failure," HIS, Feb. 1976.
J. I. Packer, *Knowing God* (IVP, 1973), pp. 221-29.

6 / Sin and
Christian Growth

PERSONAL INITIATIVE
VERSUS PASSIVITY / DAY 7

PURPOSE / To see the place of personal discipline and initiative in the Christian life.

SCRIPTURE READING / I Corinthians 9:14–27 (read in modern translation); II Timothy 2:1–7

1 / What are the indications that Paul exercised initiative and self-control in

his ministry?   (I Corinthians)_____

_____

_____

_____

2 / How was Paul an example of the three illustrations in II Timothy?____

_____

_____

SUMMARY OF TEACHING

In our struggle against sin we must not only respond properly to God's discipline of us. We must also learn to discipline ourselves, to make sure we don't become spiritually weak through neglect. The Christian life is not just the practice of avoiding sin. Such a negative concept can lead to a complacent and indolent life that neglects to do good. In other words, as Christians we are not to be passive agents, merely reacting correctly to what life brings into our experience. It is true that at times we must wait to hear the voice of God and watch to see how He works before we can act. But often we must take initiative in life, seeking ways to use the abilities and opportunities that God has given us, choosing the best of many good possibilities for service, trying to discover how to apply the Word of God and do His will in our generation and place.

The Apostle Paul was a man who thoroughly disciplined himself to make sure he would serve God faithfully and always be in control of himself. He trusted that God would perform His good will; but at the same time he was continually reaching out to see how he could fulfill his commission, using his in-

95

genuity to discover new opportunities and means. This pleased God, and it still pleases Him to find us eager to use all we have in order to do His will.

MAKING THE TRUTH PERSONAL

1 / Why is it necessary for individuals to exercise ingenuity and initiative in the attempt to evangelize students on campus? in the dorm?_____

_____

_____

2 / List at least four of the measures you take to keep yourself disciplined and spiritually "in shape":_____

_____

_____

_____

_____

PERSONAL REACTIONS / questions, commitments, prayer requests

SUGGESTIONS FOR FURTHER STUDY
TEXTS / Philippians 2:12, 13; Luke 19:11-27; 2 Timothy 1:6, 7
LITERATURE / Howard Guinness, *Sacrifice* (IVP, 1975)
John White, *The Cost of Commitment* (IVP, 1976)

7 / Faith, Doubt, and Assurance

INTRODUCTION / DAY 1

SCRIPTURE READING / Psalm 118

There is confusion among both Christians and non-Christians about the nature of faith. Some believe that faith is an optimistic attitude toward life in general, an unwillingness to be cast down by difficulties. Others consider it an innate capacity for belief that you either have or don't have. (In this scheme an unbeliever isn't capable of becoming a believer, and no moral value is attached to either position. It is rather like being either tall or short.) Still other people regard faith as a matter of auto-suggestion or superstition, the power to convince yourself that the unreal is true by basing your conviction on intuition rather than on factual evidence.

Within Christian thinking, faith is not a discrete entity that exists by itself. It is essentially a response to something known to be true, response to God's revelation and to God. Christians don't possess faith, they exercise it. Faith is seen in action; hence it is more than assent to certain truths. It is a commitment of trust and obedience that involves the whole personality.

Christians speak of being weak in faith or of having little faith, and some are unsure of how to grow in faith. They try to believe with greater earnestness, but find that their confidence isn't increased that way. This week we will look at the biblical definition of faith, and see some of the bases for assurance, growth in faith, and means of combating disbelief.

ASSIGNMENT

1 / Ask four friends what they believe faith is, and why they do or don't exercise it. Note their answers. At the end of the week evaluate the answers for accuracy and validity on the basis of scriptural teaching.

2 / Before Day Four make a note of any problems that cause you to doubt God's existence or the truth or reliability of Scripture. If you have ideas about how to overcome your doubts, write them down. Re-check your list after studying Days Four through Seven to see if your Bible reading has helped answer some of your questions.

PURPOSE / To see what true Christian faith is and how it is expressed in action.

SCRIPTURE READING / Hebrews 11:1–6, 13–16; II Corinthians 4:16–18

1 / What two aspects of faith are necessary in order to please God?   (Hebrews)_____

_____

2 / How does faith affect the Christian's view of life and the world? (II Corinthians)_____

_____

_____How does this

explain the attitude of the people of faith in Hebrews 11:13?_____

_____

_____

_____

SUMMARY OF TEACHING

Christian faith can never properly be considered apart from an understanding of who God is, because faith never exists apart from its Object.   Christian faith means choosing to look at life and act in it on the basis that God is who He says He is, that truth (including truth about me) is what He proclaims it to be, that He will do what He has promised, and that He will always act according to His character as He has revealed it.   More briefly, faith is obedience based on what I know of God and His truth.

The strength and quality of our faith, then, is directly related to our concept of God.   That is, it is in proportion to what we know and believe about Him. The way to grow in faith is not to try to believe more intensely, but to enlarge our understanding of God's Person by studying His self-revelation in Scripture, and by proving His character in experience. "Faith comes by hearing, and hearing by the word of God." If our faith is small, it is because our God is too small. We must think magnificently of our God if we are to think truly of Him. Then our faith will assume right proportions.

Our understanding of God must not only be of who He is, but of what He can do. To please Him we must believe that *He is,* and that *He rewards* those who seek Him diligently.

MAKING THE TRUTH PERSONAL

1 / If you exercise faith in God, how should your attitude toward your current economic status and future occupational success show it?_____

_____

_____

_____

2 / How does today's reading help you understand why your faith has been weak at times?_____

_____

_____

3 / What two ingredients are essential to your growth in faith?_____

_____

_____

PERSONAL REACTIONS / questions, commitments, prayer requests

SUGGESTIONS FOR FURTHER STUDY
TEXTS / Genesis 12:1-9 and Romans 4:13-25 (example of Abraham)
LITERATURE / J. A. Motyer, *The Tests of Faith* (IVP, 1970)
John White, *The Fight* (IVP, 1976), pp. 97-119.

PURPOSE / To see what facts give us confidence that our faith is rightly placed in God.

SCRIPTURE READING / John 5:24; I John 2:1–6; Romans 8:31–39

1 / What evidences in these passages assure us that we have eternal life from

God?_____

_____

_____

_____

_____

SUMMARY OF TEACHING

Our faith necessarily involves trust in what is unseen, confidence that the visible is transient and the invisible eternal. This fact sometimes raises problems for us, since what can be seen presses in on us with overwhelming insistence, and unseen spiritual realities seem elusive or incapable of proof. The question then may arise: how do we know that our faith is properly placed, that we really know God and have eternal life?

The Scriptures point us to facts by which we can test ourselves and see why we can be confident in God's working. Among them are these:

a / The statement by Jesus that those who believe in Him have eternal life and will not come into judgment.

b / The character of the work Jesus Christ did for us. As the perfect Sacrifice, His death was sufficient to take away the sins of the world. Because He died for us while we were still sinners, we can be confident of His love.

c / The Father's response to Jesus' sacrifice in raising Him from the dead. God accounts us righteous because of Jesus' merit and payment for sin when we put our trust in Him.

d / The work Jesus Christ now does for us. Not only is He the Author of our faith; He will complete it. He is at the right hand of the Father interceding for us continually on the basis of His merit.

e / The Holy Spirit, who has come to dwell in us and to bear witness that we are children of God.

f / The witness of our changed character and behavior. Our obedience to the commands of God and our love for other Christians tells us that our knowledge of God is real and that we are abiding in Him.

g / The claim of Scripture that nothing can separate us from the love of God, and Jesus' statement that no one can snatch us out of His hand.

MAKING THE TRUTH PERSONAL

1 / The Scriptures tell us (II Corinthians 13:5) to examine ourselves to see whether we are in the Faith. What evidence assures you that you have been born of God?_____

_____

_____

_____

2 / What is the place of feelings among biblical evidences of assurance that you have forgiveness and eternal life?_____

_____

PERSONAL REACTIONS / questions, commitments, prayer requests

SUGGESTIONS FOR FURTHER STUDY

TEXTS / John 10:27-30; Romans 5:1-11; 8:14-17; Hebrews 7:23-27; 9:24-26; Job 19: 25-27; Psalm 27
LITERATURE / Os Guinness, *In Two Minds* (IVP, 1976)

7 / Faith, Doubt, and Assurance

PURPOSE / To see the nature of Satan's work against believers, and to learn what God has provided for withstanding his attacks.

SCRIPTURE READING / I Peter 5:6–9; Ephesians 6:10–18

1 / In what kind of a battle is the Christian involved?_____

_____

_____

2 / What weapons has God made available for the battle? Which are defensive, and which offensive?_____

_____

SUMMARY OF TEACHING

The young Christian soon discovers that he is involved in a great spiritual battle in which Satan and his forces are pitted against God and His Church. Knowing that he has already been defeated by Jesus Christ in His death and resurrection, Satan employs his chief tactic of deceit to keep believers as well as unbelievers from seeing the truth and to cause them to believe lies. Satan has achieved his purpose if he can deceive Christians into thinking that their cause is lost, develop in them a minority complex, and convince them that there is no battle. Thus he causes them to sink into despair, resignation, or complacency, and as a result, desist from the struggle against sin and Satan.

Satan will try to get believers to focus attention on their own strengths and weaknesses instead of on Jesus Christ and His victory. He will take advantage of a person who is physically or emotionally weary, and the one who lacks self-control. His attacks will cause self-centeredness, discouragement, depression, hopelessness, and lack of faith. He will try to deceive believer and nonbeliever alike by posing as a messenger of truth and light while bearing a false gospel that leads only to bondage and death.

The Christian can be equipped with God's armor to withstand Satan. He must put on truth, righteousness, the gospel of peace, faith, and salvation. To wage war offensively, the Christian has the sword of the Spirit (the Word of God) and prayer. Jesus showed the use of God's Word in defeating Satan when

He was tempted (Matthew 4:1–11). Since the devil's plan is to deceive, blind, and slander, the Christian must know God's Word thoroughly in order to discern rightly, and behave in such a manner that any slander of him will be seen to be spurious.

MAKING THE TRUTH PERSONAL

1 / Describe the condition of the Christian when he is most susceptible to Satan's attacks._____

_____

_____

2 / How can you best prepare yourself not to be deceived by Satan's attacks?

_____

_____

_____What are you doing specifically?

_____

PERSONAL REACTIONS / questions, commitments, prayer requests

SUGGESTIONS FOR FURTHER STUDY
TEXTS / 2 Corinthians 4:3, 4; 10:3, 4; 11:14-15; Colossians 2:13-15; 2 Thessalonians 2:9, 10; Job 1:6-12; 2:1-10
LITERATURE / John White, *The Fight* (IVP, 1976), pp. 77-96.

7 / Faith, Doubt, and Assurance

PURPOSE / To see how man's willfulness can lead him to disbelief.

SCRIPTURE READING / Romans 1:18–23; John 7:14–19

1 / How did the men discussed in Romans 1 treat the truth they knew about God?_____

_____

What was the result?_____

2 / How did Jesus say that one could know whether His teaching was from God?_____

_____(Why did the Pharisees disbelieve Him?)_____

_____

SUMMARY OF TEACHING

Every man has enough evidence from the world around him and from personal experience to know that there is a God. The common reaction of men, however, is to ignore this truth, deny it, suppress it, so that they can do what they want. Their declaration of independence from God can only result in the darkening of their moral and intellectual understanding. Having exchanged truth for a lie, they express their attitude by worshiping various created things and indulging in debauched, forbidden behavior. Having started with a knowledge of the truth, they end in a state of slavery to their passions and of blindness through willful disbelief.

Jesus said that the way to discover whether He is the Truth is to will to do God's will; the truth will then be made plain. Christians must beware of resisting God. Disobedience can only result in their understanding being darkened. Obedience brings light and understanding. One of the basic causes of doubt in the Christian's life is his refusal to obey God in an issue where God's will is clear. The path back to light is repentance and obedience. Faith results.

MAKING THE TRUTH PERSONAL

1 / Are you aware of anything that God wants you to do, or not do, in which you have not obeyed Him yet? Name it (them)._____

_____

_____

What can you expect to result if you persist in disobedience?_____

_____

Ask God for grace to desire to do His will and know His truth.

2 / How does this reading help you understand why some of your friends might not believe in Jesus Christ?_____

_____

How should you pray for them?_____

_____

PERSONAL REACTIONS / questions, commitments, prayer requests

SUGGESTIONS FOR FURTHER STUDY
LITERATURE / Os Guinness, *In Two Minds* (IVP, 1976), pp. 121-37.

PURPOSE / To see how feelings affect our ability to judge facts.

SCRIPTURE READING / I Kings 19:1–18; II Corinthians 1:8–10

1 / What caused Elijah to lose confidence?_____

_____

_____

Contrast this with the situation in I Kings 18:36–40.
2 / How was Elijah restored to a right view of the truth?_____

_____

_____

SUMMARY OF TEACHING

Emotions can be both a delightful and devastating complement to our intellectual appreciation of life. They are notoriously unreliable because they are affected by factors unrelated to the matters they judge (even such factors as weather, diet, health, people's reactions, world conditions).

The case of Elijah is a good example. In a great test of authority, God used Elijah conclusively to demonstrate His reality and the falseness of Baal worship. Elijah had been through an exhausting experience, but in the exultation of victory he further wasted his strength (18:46). A threat on his life by the queen, the patroness of the Baal-priests, brought an emotional reaction of panic that caused Elijah to ask God to let him die. He bathed himself in self-pity, feeling neglected, alone in his fight against idolatry and devotion to God, useless, and finished. God recognized the roots of the problem and met Elijah's need. First of all, He solved the problem of physical exhaustion by making him eat and sleep. Then the Lord reminded Elijah of His presence and power, gave him another job to do, and revealed that He had many others who stood with Elijah in his devotion to God and opposition to sin. Elijah recovered.

We must likewise recognize the source of deceitful feelings, and understand that the physical, emotional, and spiritual are intimately related. We should provide for proper physical and mental health, and not allow ourselves to overlook the unchanging objective nature of God's truth and providence. Doubt will disappear when we focus our attention on God and exercise physical and emotional self-control. We can do this, because He has won the victory which is ours to claim.

MAKING THE TRUTH PERSONAL

1 / How can you evaluate a situation from God's point of view to see whether or not your feelings about it are accurate reactions?_____

_____

_____

2 / Do you know yourself well enough to recognize what factors (the weather, for instance, or the prospect of a difficult job) affect your feelings and attitudes, and how they do?_____

What can you do now to avoid having your outlook and judgment made unreliable by such feelings?_____

_____

_____

PERSONAL REACTIONS / questions, commitments, prayer requests

SUGGESTIONS FOR FURTHER STUDY
TEXTS / 1 John 3:19, 20; 2 Corinthians 1:8-20; 4:6-12; 7:2-16
LITERATURE / Os Guinness, *In Two Minds* (IVP, 1976), pp. 153-68.

7 / Faith, Doubt, and Assurance

PURPOSE / To see some of the reasons for our inability to understand all the facts we learn and why this causes us problems of doubt.

SCRIPTURE READING / Psalm 73

1 / What conflicting thoughts and facts caused Asaph's problem (vss. 1–3, 13–16)?_____

_____

_____

2 / What change caused his problem to be resolved (vss. 16–20)?_____

_____

_____

SUMMARY OF TEACHING

Because men are rational creatures they want to be able to reduce all truth to logical systems of thought. As a Christian student sharpens his mental abilities and is confronted with a vastly enlarged world of facts and ideas in the university, he sometimes encounters intellectual problems. These are caused by facts, or interpretations of facts, that seem inconsistent with his biblical view of the world. Or they may be problems that arise for him within the scope of biblical teaching, where he cannot fit all the facts together logically. As a result he begins to question the validity of the truth revealed in Scripture; or else he tries to disprove the facts that seem to disagree with revelation. Or he may decide not to try to resolve the problem at all, trusting in "faith" rather than in reason.

In Psalm 73 Asaph had a problem. He believed that God was true, and that obedience to Him was the right course for life. But the facts seemed to disprove his faith. The wicked prospered and the righteous suffered. He agonized over the paradox, torn between the desire to remain true to God and the need to face the facts. His problem wasn't resolved until he recognized that God will not completely vindicate His standard of righteousness until a future day of reckoning. Asaph first had to come into the presence of God and look at life from His point of view; then his problem was resolved.

We cannot run away from the intellectual problems we meet in life. God is the God of truth, and a dishonest or cowardly attitude toward any area of His truth cannot please Him. We need to learn why facts sometimes seem contradictory, and we must also learn right approaches to them. Some basic principles relating to intellectual problems of doubt are discussed in the *addendum* following today's reading.

MAKING THE TRUTH PERSONAL

1 / As you face intellectual problems that puzzle you or challenge your faith, how can you demonstrate your conviction that Jesus Christ is the Truth, and

that in Him "are hid all the treasures of wisdom and knowledge"?_____

_____

_____

_____

_____

Pray for the ability to see basic principles in the problems you have and to understand God's Word in such a way that you will reach right conclusions.

PERSONAL REACTIONS / questions, commitments, prayer requests

SUGGESTIONS FOR FURTHER STUDY
TEXTS / Deuteronomy 29:29; Isaiah 55:8, 9; 1 Corinthians 2; 13:12; Romans 1:20, 21; 2 Corinthians 4:18; Luke 7:19-23 (example of John the Baptist)
LITERATURE / Os Guinness, *In Two Minds* (IVP, 1976), pp. 83-119.

7 / Faith, Doubt, and Assurance

ADDENDUM

If we don't recognize some of the sources of our intellectual problems, we won't be able to solve them and we may be tempted to disbelieve as Asaph was.

The Scriptures reveal God's truth to us insofar as we can grasp it. Because God is infinite and eternal, existing outside the bounds of time and space, we who are limited by both time and space cannot fully grasp His truth. We are incapable of reducing infinite (supra-spatial), eternal (supra-temporal) truth into a finite, temporal system of thought. For this reason we will not be able fully to comprehend the relation of God's sovereignty to man's responsibility, or the mystery of the infinite God becoming a man, or the greater mystery of the Source of life dying for the sake of His creatures.

God has not yet revealed all truth to us. We know that in His Word He has given us all the truth we need in order to do His will, but there are still hidden things that He alone knows (Deuteronomy 29:29). This was true even for Jesus in His self-imposed limitation as a man. (Note what He said in Mark 13:32 about the time of the final Day of the Lord.)

Occasionally Christians are disturbed because the Bible is silent on some troublesome matter of science, and they wonder if perhaps their faith is outmoded, if the God of the Bible has been bypassed in the progress of modern scientific discovery. They fail to see that the purpose of the Bible is not to give a full scientific explanation of the world. It is the account of God's acts in relation to His plan for the world in general and His people in particular; and therefore, although the Scripture speaks accurately, it omits many tantalizing details because they are not necessary to the account (for example, the methods God used in creation).

Sometimes we are confronted with facts, the full implications of which we cannot grasp. Thus we are incapable of synthesizing them into our understanding of life, history, theology, or science. This may be a testimony to the limitation of our capacity to understand, or an evidence of faulty understanding of what Scripture says. Or it may indicate that all the facts in the subject have not yet been uncovered or presented. In any case, just as we do in any field of study, we should be willing to withhold final judgment until further light is given from Scripture, history, or scientific studies. The problem can be further complicated when we are taught facts along with interpretations made by men whose philosophies are basically atheistic. It is difficult for laymen to distinguish between facts and interpretations in many fields, and to tell whether the evidence cited is sufficient to warrant the conclusions made. In cases where the interpretation is doubtful, we will have to question a scholar in the field to see if the facts justify some meaning that has been set forth.

Conclusions seemingly contrary to Scripture often are presented before all the facts have been considered or uncovered. As new facts and insights have emerged, the history of science and philosophy shows several revolutions in thought. This should caution us not to adopt particular views of facts unsubstantiated by Scripture to say something it did not intend (such as Bishop Usshur's date for creation, or the theory of a geocentric universe).

We may encounter problems of understanding if we attempt to judge the truth by the experiences of life rather than by God's Word as it illuminates life. This was Asaph's problem. Much of God's truth will not be vindicated publicly until He finally judges men. We may be able to accept the problems of evil, suffering, and rewards in this life, but we will not be able fully to understand them until that day; and until then they will continue to plague many men's understanding.

Christianity is not illogical, irrational or anti-intellectual. But only those who have been enlightened by the Holy Spirit can understand God's wisdom; and even for them understanding God's truth comes through obedience and a knowledge of His Word that is proved in experience. God has given us enough knowledge to know Him and grow in grace despite the problems we face. We don't have all the answers, but we have enough.

SCRIPTURE READING / Ephesians 1:3–14

Many Christians regard the process of knowing God's will as difficult and perplexing. And yet Jesus taught us to pray, "Thy will be done on earth as it is in heaven," with the expectation that our prayer will be answered. Apparently God sees His will as a practical goal that Christians can achieve daily.

For many individuals the practice of discovering God's will has been obscured by a type of teaching that implies that there is a set pattern of rules for guidance to be followed. We cannot restrict God in such a way; nor do Scriptures warrant it. God guides in different ways at different times for different people. He does this so that we will not depend on formulas of guidance but on Him. God is the changeless factor in guidance, and He will guide. If we look steadily to Him for wisdom we cannot be disappointed. But we cannot expect His direction if we lose contact with Him and look to other means of help. He has made this clear: "I will guide thee with mine eye" (Psalm 32:8). As a father can indicate his pleasure or disapproval to his child through a glance because of their closeness, so God guides us.

Often we don't like to make decisions, and would rather that life "happened" automatically by God's rigging circumstances, or by others' choices. The mark of Christian maturity, however, is to exercise the discernment that God has given us. As we learn to know His mind through the teaching of the Spirit and His Word, we will be able to see God's guidance in the practical issues of life and will act decisively in faith.

ASSIGNMENT

Evaluate the following three situations in writing. Why or why not are the reasons given valid? What other factors should be taken into account?

1 / You have the opportunity and funds ($300) to buy a good secondhand car during the school year. Since you want a car, have enough money in your account, and this car is available, it is God's will for you to buy it.

2 / During the second semester of your sophomore year you must choose a major field of study. You decide on a curriculum because your parents want you to choose that major, and they're paying your way through school.

113

3 / You must decide whether to live in the college dorms or in a single room off campus next year.   Since few Christians live in the dorm, and since you will have greater opportunities for witness there because of the number of students, you decide on the dorm.

PURPOSE / To see what it means to know the will of God, and how this is related to guidance.

SCRIPTURE READING / I Thessalonians 4:1–8; Isaiah 58:6–12

1 / With what does Paul equate the will of God?_____

_____How does one show he knows the will of

God?_____

_____

2 / What did Isaiah tell the Jewish people to do in order to have divine guidance and provision?_____

_____

How do you assure yourself of having guidance from God?_____

_____

SUMMARY OF TEACHING

It is curious that Christians today are preoccupied with guidance and discovering the will of God, when the Scriptures say so little about how to uncover the specific details of God's plan for an individual's life. Rather, the Bible emphasizes that the believer should seek holiness, being obedient to what he knows he should do. Guidance is not a goal to be sought; it is a fact of experience promised to those who obey God.

God has made His will plain in the Bible. His will for us is sanctification, which means growing in holiness of character, becoming more like Jesus Christ. God's will for us does involve specific choices: vocation, life partner, location, purchases, friendships, and so on. But those choices must be made in the course of consistent living according to God's Word. Our faithfulness in obeying the commands and prohibitions of Scripture in the present is far more pleasing to God than our ability to foresee the details of future choices in life.

God is the goal and meaning of our life. A steady desire to know Him, to be like Him, and to please Him by our service, should characterize our lives rather than great agitation to wheedle from Him facts about our future. We can rest in the assurance that His concern for our future is greater than ours, and that His promise is true: "I will instruct thee and teach thee in the way which thou shalt go; I will guide thee with mine eye" (Psalm 32:8).

MAKING THE TRUTH PERSONAL

1 / About what specific future choices in life are you concerned to know

God's will?_____

Are you willing to believe He will guide you to right decisions as you concern

yourself with knowing and obeying Him more fully in daily living?_____

_____Commit these things to the Lord and thank Him for

His promise of guidance.

PERSONAL REACTIONS / questions, commitments, prayer requests

SUGGESTIONS FOR FURTHER STUDY
TEXTS / Ephesians 1:3-14; Proverbs 3:5, 6; Psalm 48:14
LITERATURE / *HIS Essays on Guidance* (IVP, 1968)
Paul Little, *Affirming the Will of God* (IVP, 1971)
J. I. Packer, *Knowing God* (IVP, 1973), pp. 209-20.

PURPOSE / To see what kind of person God promises to guide.

SCRIPTURE READING / Psalm 25:1–15; James 1:5–8

1 / Describe the man guided by God (vss. 4, 5, 8–10, 12, 14)._____

_____

_____

_____

_____

(Note that God's guidance is directly related to His Word: "His covenant and His testimonies.")

2 / According to James, what deprives men of divine wisdom in the face of

trials?_____

_____

SUMMARY OF TEACHING

God does not promise guidance for all men. The Bible makes clear that certain attitudes of heart characterize those who can perceive His leading.

God wants to know that we trust Him implicitly, that we believe He is the source of wisdom and the One whose ways are right. He is pleased when we desire His insight, rather than relying on our own wisdom or being ready to debate His. We must admit that our understanding is not sufficient or completely true. He will not show His ways to those whose motive is to use Him for selfish ends. Our asking must show that we want God to be God and ourselves His servants.

If we ask for wisdom while persisting in disobedience, or if we ask without expecting to obey (e.g., if we disagree with God's view), we won't receive insight. God takes no pleasure in fools (Ecclesiastes 5:4), and is willing to give guidance only to those who acknowledge His right to control every area of life. If we are not trying to obey what we already know to be right, we need not ask for further light. A double-minded man will receive nothing from the Lord. But He delights in giving friendship and guidance to those who fear Him.

MAKING THE TRUTH PERSONAL

1 / How does today's reading help you understand why guidance may not have been clear in past or current decisions?_____

_____

_____

2 / In what areas are you tempted to disobey guidance that runs contrary to your own desires?_____

_____

_____How can you be sure that God will enable you to decide?_____

_____

_____

PERSONAL REACTIONS / questions, commitments, prayer requests

SUGGESTIONS FOR FURTHER STUDY
TEXTS / Psalm 32:8-10; Proverbs 3:5-8; Psalm 66:18
LITERATURE / Alan Redpath, *Getting to Know the Will of God* (IVP, 1954)

PURPOSE / To see what guidance is and what factors are involved in discovering it.

SCRIPTURE READING / Proverbs 2:1–15; II Timothy 3:14–17

1 / What are the practical results of receiving God's wisdom?_____

_____

_____

_____

2 / What results has God's Word had in your life?   (Give two specific examples.)_____

_____

_____

SUMMARY OF TEACHING

We must seek God's guidance primarily from the teaching of Scripture. His Word contains all the understanding we need in order to do His will (see Deuteronomy 29:29). This does not mean the Christian should expect to find every conceivable situation or decision in life described in the Bible. Nor does it imply that God intends to provide direction through the chance selection of Scripture verses or situations. We are to study the Bible as a whole so that we learn to view life from God's point of view.

How can we know God's point of view? We must learn from the Scriptures what He commands and proscribes. We must discover what God desires for the world, the individual, and His Church. We must seek the reasons that God has given for His actions in the world. And we should see how men of the Bible applied His truth to life. The Holy Spirit reveals the mind of God to us (see I Corinthians 2:6 ff.), and so we must ask Him to make plain the meaning and application of scriptural truth. We cannot discover it without Him. By such study we will learn the principles we need in order to judge life as we ought.

The Lord has promised to give us wisdom and counsel, that is, the ability to understand and apply His truth in specific decisions of life. This does not relieve us of the responsibility to investigate facts carefully and use our minds; but it does promise us that we will be able to judge correctly when seeking to know the way of obedience in a situation. He has provided teachers, books, and friends to give us counsel, but their authority springs from their ability to apply scriptural principles to life. We should use such counsel gratefully, being sure to weigh it against the Word of God. To know the will of God we must know the Word of God: "Then shalt thou understand righteousness, and judgment, and equity; yea, and every good path."

MAKING THE TRUTH PERSONAL

1 / List several scriptural principles that should guide you in making major

decisions, such as choosing a vocation. _____

_____

_____

_____

_____

2 / Why is it important to know God's point of view on marriage when making

decisions about your campus social life? _____

_____

_____

_____

PERSONAL REACTIONS / questions, commitments, prayer requests

SUGGESTIONS FOR FURTHER STUDY
TEXTS / 1 Corinthians 2; Hebrews 5:11-14; Proverbs 12:15
LITERATURE / John White, *The Fight* (IVP, 1976), pp. 153-77.

PURPOSE / To see how factors other than the Scriptures affect our understanding of divine guidance.

SCRIPTURE READING / Acts 4:13–31

1 / How might the apostles have acted if they had relied on circumstances and feelings in this incident?_____

_____

_____Why did they act differently than might be expected?_____

_____

2 / How would you have reacted to the council's order if you had been Peter or John?_____

_____

SUMMARY OF TEACHING

Because we know that God is active in all of life, sustaining, providing, and protecting, we believe that things do not happen to us by chance and without meaning. This has led some Christians, in seeking to know God's will, to give undue weight to the significance of various factors of their environment: the appearance of individuals, opportunities, the weather, personal abilities, people's reactions, coincidental happenings, possessions. Such Christians look on these factors as special "signs" or indications of how to make decisions.

To be sure, we must consider circumstances when we make choices. God can use them to hinder our acting or to enable us to choose when conditions please Him. But our decisions still must be based on scriptural principles, not merely on the opportunity to act, or on hunches. In the Bible we see men both using or ignoring circumstances because they acted on principles and evaluated circumstances in light of them.

Again, some Christians lay great emphasis on an inner sense of peace or rightness as the sign of a right decision. God has promised to give us peace, and we should thank Him for it; but He has not promised to guide us by our feelings. Decision-making is often an emotion-charged experience, and many Christians must choose in the midst of personal turmoil. As we become convinced that we have acted in accordance with the Word of God, He may give inner calm. But our confidence must be in God and His truth, not in our emotional response to life.

MAKING THE TRUTH PERSONAL

1 / How can you evaluate the significance of circumstances when making a choice (e.g., the offer of an out-of-town job with good pay at the time you are looking for summer employment)?_____

_____

_____

2 / Why might your feelings be unreliable when you consider the possibility of starting an evangelistic Bible study in your dorm?_____

_____

What factors would be more important in making that decision?_____

_____

_____

PERSONAL REACTIONS / questions, commitments, prayer requests

SUGGESTIONS FOR FURTHER STUDY
LITERATURE / John White, *The Fight* (IVP, 1976), pp. 153-77.

PURPOSE / To see how one can decide what the will of God is in a specific situation.

SCRIPTURE READING / Acts 15:1–29

1 / What methods did the apostles and elders use in deciding the will of God in the matter of circumcising Gentiles (vss. 4–7, 12–15, 19, 20, 22, 23)?

_____

_____

2 / How did they regard their decision (vs. 28)?_____

_____

SUMMARY OF TEACHING

To make decisions we need to know the available facts of the situation, possible alternatives of choice, and applicable scriptural principles. Having weighed them carefully, we should try to come to the most reasonable conclusion about how God is guiding.

One of the aspects of God's providence is that He may withhold information that would cause us to decide differently than He desires (e.g., another and more attractive job opportunity). We should trust that He will allow us sufficient information to make right decisions as we apply the Spirit-given wisdom of His Word to the facts. On the other hand, we may limit God in His guidance by restricting the possibilities we consider. If we do not expose ourselves to information about foreign missions, for example, it is unlikely that we will decide to serve God as a missionary. And if we refuse to consider any other profession than teaching, it is predictable that we will end up as a teacher.

Feelings must be considered, especially if they indicate the possibility of disobedience. By themselves they should not cause us to make or change a decision, but they should lead us to rethink the situation and the reasons for our conclusions. Then we must act, either in agreement or disagreement with our feelings, on the basis of scriptural behavior.

We do not negate one area of responsibility by assuming another. The choice of a vocation to work with things does not relieve us of the duty to witness

to people. Leaving home to marry does not excuse us from honoring our parents.
Decisions must be made within the total context of God's truth. Having made a
decision, we should hold to it in faith unless new factors clearly contrary to
Scripture arise, which would make persistence in it sin. We should expect so to
grow in a balanced understanding of the counsels of God that our reactions to life
will begin to show that we have adopted God's point of view; then every decision
will not require great investigation.

MAKING THE TRUTH PERSONAL

1 / How are you preparing to make certain that your major decisions in the
next few years (vocation, further education, marriage, location) will be in the will

of God?_____

_____

_____

2 / How can you avoid limiting the scope of God's guidance in any of those

areas?_____

_____

PERSONAL REACTIONS / questions, commitments, prayer requests

SUGGESTIONS FOR FURTHER STUDY
TEXTS / 1 Corinthians 16:3-12; 2 Corinthians 1:15—2:4
LITERATURE / Tim Stafford, "Thy Will Be Known," HIS, Mar. 1975.
Alan Redpath, *Getting to Know the Will of God* (IVP, 1954)

PURPOSE / To see that the will of God for Christians includes the work of world evangelism.

SCRIPTURE READING / Romans 10:11–17; Matthew 28:18–20; Philippians 2:19–24

1 / Describe God's plan for making sure that all men will be able to believe in Him._____

_____

2 / Why was Timothy more commendable than the other Christians?_____

_____

_____

SUMMARY OF TEACHING

Jesus said that the Church must proclaim the gospel throughout the world and make disciples of all nations (including our own). Yet many Christians look on God's program of world evangelism as the hobby of a few missions enthusiasts. But for the true believer the question is not "world evangelism: yes or no?" but "world evangelism: where and how?"

God does not force people to serve Him; He gives them freedom to obey or disobey. Many Christians refuse to consider personal involvement in missionary work, and others keep themselves ignorant of the conditions and needs around the world. The problem is not new. The Apostle Paul wrote about the self-interest that kept Christians from serving others, and noted the consequent lack of concerned workers to meet obvious needs.

If we are honest we will ask God how we may take part in evangelizing our generation. Taking into consideration the gifts He has given us, our training, the counsel of others, and areas of need, we must investigate the possibilities of service. He will give us concern, He will structure circumstances, and enable us to judge where and how we should serve Him. Overseas missionary service is not the hallmark of highest spirituality. But it is a much-neglected possibility of showing our obedience and love to the Lord, who appoints His children to the most appropriate places of service. We must let Him decide.

MAKING THE TRUTH PERSONAL

1 / What action are you taking to discover the conditions and needs of foreign missionary work in specific countries?   (Name the countries.)_____

_____

_____

_____

2 / How are you going to find out if God wants you to serve Him as a missionary overseas?_____

_____

_____

_____

PERSONAL REACTIONS / questions, commitments, prayer requests

SUGGESTIONS FOR FURTHER STUDY
TEXTS / Acts 1:8; 2 Corinthians 5:14-21; Matthew 9:35-38
LITERATURE / Michael Griffiths, *You and God's Work Overseas* (IVP, 1967)
Martin Goldsmith, *Don't Just Stand There* (IVP, 1976)
Ralph Winter, *Say Yes to Mission* (IVP, 1970)

SCRIPTURE READING / II Thessalonians 1

Today as the ecumenical movement captures the concern and energy of many churches, the doctrine of the Church is of great theological interest. Other factors also have focused attention on biblical teaching in this area: the emergence of different patterns of organization, worship, and fellowship in young non-Western churches; the self-examination of basic purposes and methods by churches confronting the attacks of totalitarian forces; and the questions of strategy and goals for the missionary movement in a modern world. But before you can think critically in such areas, you must look at yourself in relation to the Christians with whom you live and work from day to day.

A right understanding of the Church and its work, and how the individual is related to it, must underlie Christian growth in maturity and the intelligent exercise of spiritual gifts, for God works out His will on earth through the Church. Although the Scriptures speak of the necessity of a personal relationship with God, they never imply that the Christian is not an active part of the larger body. In fact, the Bible teaches that one cannot do the work of God apart from it.

An Inter-Varsity chapter is not a local church, but rather a temporary fellowship of Christians drawn from many churches and banded together for purposes of evangelism, fellowship, and spiritual growth. Many of the activities of a local church are appropriately carried on in an Inter-Varsity chapter (i.e., prayer, Bible study, teaching, fellowship, meeting one another's needs, witnessing —see Acts 2:41–47), while others are not (e.g., baptism, communion, marriage, excommunication). In order for Christians to express the life of Jesus Christ on the campus, they should understand what the Bible teaches about the Church.

What are the simple facts (as they affect daily life) of one Christian's relationship to other Christians? In trying to understand these facts we shall look at Scriptures that teach about the believers' unity in Christ, which is expressed within the framework of the diverse functions given each individual in the Church. We will see that love must be the motivating principle for all activity within the Body of Christ, and that the fellowship of Christians together is actually the sharing of a common life. Within a group of divergent and not-yet-perfect believers, problems will always arise; and so we will investigate biblical principles of resolving grievances between brothers and keeping differences of opinion from destroying fellowship and crippling growth.

ASSIGNMENT

To be done before the discussion meeting, preferably before the fourth day.

1 / Make a survey to find out what four other Christians (at least two of them not members of your discussion group) think fellowship is, and write down the definitions. Then write a paragraph giving your definition of Christian fellowship. What distinguishes it from the fellowship that non-Christians have? Can you support your answers biblically?

2 / List what you believe to be the Christian's major responsibilities to other Christians (at least five answers). How do you fulfill them? For what motives?

PURPOSE / To see how Christians are unified, and to what this unity bears
witness.

SCRIPTURE READING / John 17

1 / What did Jesus pray for His disciples? for us?_____

_____

_____

2 / Why is the unity of Christians so important in the work of evangelism?

(What does it prove?)_____

_____

_____

_____

SUMMARY OF TEACHING

At the end of His ministry Jesus taught His disciples the significance of
their relationship with one another and what their ministry in the world would
be after his departure (John 13–16). They had come to know the Father through
Jesus, and because of their obedience and identity with Him, the world hated
them and would hate them. It could not understand their life principle. They
would experience fullness of joy in Jesus in the face of conflict with the world;
and they were to bear witness to their Lord by obeying Jesus' command and
loving one another.

Then (as recorded in John 17) Jesus prayed for them, that they and those
who were to believe would be one in Him. Their unity would prove to the world
that God had sent Him, that they were loved by God, and that they were Jesus'
disciples (cf. John 13:34, 35). They would be distinguished from the world by
knowing Jesus' true identity and position; and by growing in the knowledge of
God through Jesus, they would experience and express the love of God.

MAKING THE TRUTH PERSONAL

1 / In what way has the work of God in non-Christians been strengthened by your life with other Christians? (Memorize John 13:34, 35.)_____

_____

_____

_____

_____

2 / What distinguishes you from the world? What should?_____

_____

_____

_____

PERSONAL REACTIONS / questions, commitments, prayer requests

SUGGESTIONS FOR FURTHER STUDY

TEXTS / John 13—16

LITERATURE / Francis A. Schaeffer, *The Mark of the Christian* (IVP, 1970)

9 The Christian Fellowship

DIVERSITY OF FUNCTION / DAY **3**

PURPOSE / To discover the origin and structure of the Body of Christ and learn how individuals are related to one another in its work.

SCRIPTURE READING / I Corinthians 12

1 / By noting who takes initiative in this passage, what do you learn about the origin and work of the Body?_____

_____

_____

_____

SUMMARY OF TEACHING

Jesus Christ established the Church (all who have been born anew by the Holy Spirit) to continue His work on earth. This work is extensive and varied, and requires that individuals have special, differing abilities in order to accomplish God's purposes. Members need the capacity to proclaim the gospel and bring men to repentance and faith, to provide clear teaching for the Church, to administer the affairs of the Body and maintain discipline, to provide for the spiritual and physical needs of individuals, and to carry out any other necessary work. In the superintending wisdom of God, the Holy Spirit equips each believer with a spiritual gift or gifts to meet some need in the overall work of the Church. Since all belong to the same Body and share the work, each is to use his gift for the sake of other Christians as well as for God.

Difficulties arise when some Christians think that all must be exactly alike in function, and try, therefore, either to conform to the pattern of another man's life or force others to change (everyone must witness the same way, or become the same kind of leader or counselor). Problems also arise when someone uses a Spirit-inspired gift as a basis for personal pride and disdains others, instead of recognizing that no man can take credit for what God has given him to use (ability to understand Scripture, sing or lead meetings). In God's sight each member is equally important, and equally responsible for doing his work well. (See Ephesians 4:1–17 where Paul teaches that spiritual gifts are to be used for building up the Body until it achieves maturity in being like Jesus Christ, unified, doctrinally stable, and growing in love as all parts work together.)

131

MAKING THE TRUTH PERSONAL

How will the facts studied today affect the following situations?
    1 / Choosing leaders for a Christian group. (What attitudes should both the candidates and group have?)_____

_____

_____

_____

    2 / Your attitude toward the gifts God has given you. (Do you know what they are? How are you using them? For whom? Are you dissatisfied, proud, thankful?)_____

_____

_____

_____

PERSONAL REACTIONS / questions, commitments, prayer requests

SUGGESTIONS FOR FURTHER STUDY

TEXTS / Romans 12:3-8; 1 Peter 1:22—2:10; Ephesians 4:1-16
LITERATURE / Donald Bridge and David Phypers, *Spiritual Gifts and the Church* (IVP, 1973)
T. C. Hammond, *In Understanding Be Men* (IVP, 1968), pp. 153-60.
Howard Snyder, *The Problem of Wineskins* (IVP, 1975), pp. 89-148.

PURPOSE / To see the relationship between love and the use of spiritual gifts, and to see how love behaves.

SCRIPTURE READING / I Corinthians 12:27–13:13; I John 3:10–18

1 / What does love have to do with the right use of spiritual gifts? (I Corinthians)_____

_____

Describe the effect of using them without love._____

_____

_____

2 / How can you test or demonstrate your love? (I John)_____

_____

_____

_____

SUMMARY OF TEACHING

On many occasions Jesus commanded his followers to love, and New Testament writers also insist that love characterizes all Christians' lives. We must love with the kind of love that Jesus has shown for us (John 15:12). His death for us is the greatest demonstration of love we can know. Because we have received love, we in turn are now able to give ourselves. "We love, because he first loved us" (I John 4:19).

The fact that love is *commanded* clearly shows that loving means more than having an involuntary emotional response to someone. Loving basically involves setting your will to seek another person's highest good. It is not an act of convenience; it demands a considered giving of yourself without expectation of return. As it was not easy for Jesus to love us (think what it cost Him to become a man and die), it won't be easy for us to love. (How pleasant is it to risk your reputation to befriend and help someone who is socially ostracized on your campus?) But we have the example and experience of love that enables us to give ourselves.

Having love assures us that we are children of God; its lack should cause us to question whether we know God. Love is the motive that must underlie all Christian activity. Without it, all our splendid spiritual gifts result in nothing or, possibly, in sin (see I Corinthians 8 for an example), and the work of the Body of Christ cannot be accomplished. (How could we show the life of Jesus without love? He *is* love.) The clearest statement of the way love behaves is found in I Corinthians 13:4-7. Read it in a modern translation to catch its full intent, and then paraphrase it in your own words.

MAKING THE TRUTH PERSONAL

1 / List any recent instances where you have used your God-given abilities in an impatient, unkind, irritable, rude or resentful way. How does the Scripture

evaluate such service?_____

_____

_____

_____

2 / Write down five ways in which you can show love to specific individuals

today, and ask God to help you do this._____

_____

_____

_____

PERSONAL REACTIONS / questions, commitments, prayer requests

PURPOSE / To learn what Christian fellowship is and distinguish it from other fellowships.

SCRIPTURE READING / I John 1; Acts 2:41–47

1 / Is it possible for Christians to be together and fail to have Christian fellowship? Why? (What is the basis for Christian fellowship?)_____

_____

_____

_____

2 / What breaks fellowship?_____

_____

How can it be restored?_____

_____

SUMMARY OF TEACHING

The picture given in Scripture of the Church as a family is helpful when we consider the nature and practice of fellowship. *The New English Bible* translation of I John 1:3 defines fellowship as *"sharing* in a common life, that life which we share with the Father and His Son Jesus Christ." What we know and have experienced of Jesus Christ binds us together with others in whom the life of Jesus Christ dwells, and that relationship is called fellowship. Since all have been accepted in Christ and *He* is the binding force in our fellowship, racial, cultural, economic, and social barriers are removed (see Galatians 3:26–28). We must accept one another as God has.

As in other families, membership in God's family involves responsibilities and privileges, and our accepting them should result in our growing more like Jesus Christ, being made strong in the Faith. Among these activities are prayer, study, and worship together; teaching the truth from Scripture and experience to one another; sharing personal blessings and problems (rejoicing and weeping together); encouraging, rebuking, correcting, and disciplining those who need it; and providing for the physical needs of others.

Fellowship is broken by sin, but God provides a remedy: confession and forgiveness. The source of Christian fellowship is the individual's relationship to the Lord; we must first have fellowship with Him in order to share His life with others.

MAKING THE TRUTH PERSONAL

1 / Evaluate the time you have spent with other Christians in the last week. How well in practice have you matched the biblical definition of fellowship?

_____

_____

_____

2 / What Christians from other racial and economic backgrounds *share* life with you?_____

_____

How should your life demonstrate that all are made one in Jesus Christ?_____

_____

_____

_____

(Read Philippians 2:1–4 for some good rules for fellowship. Note Jesus' example, vss. 5–11.)

PERSONAL REACTIONS / questions, commitments, prayer requests

SUGGESTIONS FOR FURTHER STUDY
TEXTS / Romans 12; Acts 2:41-47; James 2:1-9; 3:1—4:12; 5:13-20
LITERATURE / Dietrich Bonhoeffer, *Life Together* (Harper & Row, 1954)
John White, *The Fight* (IVP, 1976), pp. 121-51.

PURPOSE / To learn the purposes of Christian discipline and see the rules laid down for resolving grievances among Christians.

SCRIPTURE READING / Matthew 18:15–22; Galatians 6:1–5

1 / On whom does the responsibility fall for initiating reconciliation between estranged Christians? _____

_____

2 / What safeguards are provided by the Lord to insure a fair hearing before openly breaking fellowship with a brother? _____

_____

_____

SUMMARY OF TEACHING

God is concerned not only that His children be united, but that as a body they uphold the truth. Consequently, the Church is responsible to see that sin is not overlooked, but that offending brothers are brought to repentance and restoration when their actions are destroying fellowship. Discipline is not to be enforced hastily or in a spirit of vindictiveness but in humility, with care being taken to hear the matter fairly. Its exercise is commanded in order to protect the spiritual vitality of the body, to impress on the members the importance of obedience to the Lord, to keep an erring brother from continuing in sin, and to restore him to fellowship through forgiveness.

An Inter-Varsity chapter is not a local church, and does not exercise the prerogatives of such a body, which include baptism, communion, and excommunication (denying fellowship and communion to a brother persisting in sin). Although a chapter cannot exercise the authority of Church discipline, it must teach and encourage the practice of those spiritual duties that all Christians share. If the members act biblically, offenses that arise within their fellowship will be corrected. Maintaining open fellowship by confessing sin, going to one who has sinned, and by bearing others' burdens in humility and love, is a responsibility of all.

Many matters can be resolved if the offended person will have the honesty, love, and spiritual concern to tell the problem to his offending brother. Neglect of this practice leads to misunderstanding, gossip, harboring of resentment, toleration of sin, and spiritual deterioration. True love will always seek the spiritual rehabilitation of a brother. "Love . . . does not gloat over other men's sins, but delights in the truth" (I Corinthians 13:6, NEB).

MAKING THE TRUTH PERSONAL

1 / Are you harboring resentment against some Christian who has offended you?_____

What is your spiritual responsibility in the matter?_____

_____

2 / How can attempted disciplinary action be sinful and lead to worse results?_____

_____

_____

What motives are justified?_____

_____

What should you do if you feel like "telling off" or exposing some erring fellow Christian, but suspect that your motive is really spiritual self-justification?

PERSONAL REACTIONS / questions, commitments, prayer requests

SUGGESTIONS FOR FURTHER STUDY

TEXTS / Romans 16:17-20; 1 Corinthians 5:9—6:8; James 5:19-20; 2 Corinthians 6:14—7:1; 2:5-11; Titus 3:8-11; 2 Timothy 2:14-26; 1 Corinthians 1:10-15; 2 Corinthians 11, 12, 13
LITERATURE / Stephen Board, "All in the Family," HIS, Nov. 1972.
Charles Salter, "Restoration," HIS, Dec. 1975.
John H. Yoder, "Binding and Loosing," Concern, Feb. 1967, p. 2.

PURPOSE / To discover where Christians may have legitimate differences of opinion over doctrine and behavior, and learn how to regard such differing brothers.

SCRIPTURE READING / Romans 14:1–15:6

1 / Why is one Christian not to judge another?_____

_____

_____

What, on the other hand, are his responsibilities to other Christians?_____

_____

_____

2 / What was more important than the opinions the differing Christians

held?_____

_____

SUMMARY OF TEACHING

The Bible insists that the Christian stop sinning. When a believer breaks the clear command of Scripture he stands judged by that Scripture, and the church may discipline him.

Today confusion arises because there are many matters of social and religious practice on which the teaching of God's Word is silent or unclear (e.g. watching television, the use of liturgy). In these cases each man must decide for himself as well as he can what his behavior should be on the basis of broad scriptural principles and the guidance of the Holy Spirit, and then act out of conviction without doubting. But he is not free to condemn or dispute with another Christian whose conclusions on these matters are different. God is his judge, not his fellow believer. The Bible teaches that what one regards as sin may be lawful for another, but each must act on the basis of faith and live unto God with a good conscience.

On the other hand, we are not to be indifferent to varying standards of behavior. A mature Christian whose freedom allows him to do things that a weaker Christian considers wrong, may hurt that brother spiritually by exercising his freedom in the weaker one's presence. The rule for conduct is to recognize that we all live to glorify God (not to please ourselves), and that we must restrict ourselves even in good things where they might injure a weaker brother. His spiritual health is far more important than our pleasure. To disregard the weak is sin.

MAKING THE TRUTH PERSONAL

1 / Do you know any Christians whose religious or social behavior disturbs

you?_____ _____

Does some of your conduct disturb other brothers?_____

_____

What should you do in either case?_____

_____

_____

_____

2 / What attitudes and behavior toward those who feel freer and those who are more inhibited than you, will show that your aim in life is to glorify God

together with other believers?_____

_____

Pray that it might be so, and then act.

PERSONAL REACTIONS / questions, commitments, prayer requests

SUGGESTIONS FOR FURTHER STUDY

THOUGHT QUESTIONS / Are your standards of conduct in church and society the fruit of your own convictions from the study of God's Word, or are they a cultural heritage you have received?
What is the difference between annoying a legalist and offending a weaker brother?
LITERATURE / Paul Little, *How to Give Away Your Faith* (IVP, 1968), pp. 93-103.

140

SCRIPTURE READING / Proverbs 31

> "Three things are too wonderful for me;
>   four I do not understand:
> the way of an eagle in the sky,
>   the way of a serpent on a rock,
> the way of a ship on the high seas,
>   and the way of a man with a maiden."
>
> Proverbs 30:18, 19

Little introduction is necessary to a subject so highly stimulating to us as Christian love and marriage.   But serious and intensive consideration must be given to the subject for two reasons.   Apart from conversion, marriage is the most important single commitment an individual can make; it affects life totally and permanently.   Our society has departed so significantly from biblical teaching, and the world's influence on us is so strong, that Christians are adopting non-Christian views and practices of marriage.   We need God's perspective.

Thoughtful individuals have recognized that a large number of current social ills have their roots in maladjusted families.   Juvenile delinquency, mental illnesses, the growing problem of illegitimacy, divorce, disturbed children, suicide, homosexuality; all these spring in part from wrong relationships between husband and wife, or between parents and children.   To regain balance where there is instability, and to have an understanding of healthy family relationships so that we can look forward to establishing good homes, we need to find God's view of marriage and the family.

We can gain that perspective.   Biblical teaching in this important area is quite specific and practical.   We will consider some subjects we need to know: the origin and purpose of marriage, the proper expression of our sexual nature, the roles of husband and wife, the witness of Christian marriage in society, and the specific abuses that arise when God's Word is not heeded.   As we study these aspects of truth we can equip ourselves for living positively and enjoyably among people who have almost forgotten that God cares about our right fulfillment as men and women.

ASSIGNMENT

1 / Take a census among two or three non-Christian friends to get their answers to the following questions (write down a summary of what they say):

a / What is the purpose of marriage?

b / What do you think are the three most common motives for dating?

c / What criteria do you maintain for a possible marriage partner? (What are you looking for?)

d / Is a single life normal and/or desirable? Why or why not?

2 / Take a similar census of two or three Christian friends. Compare and contrast their answers with the first set.

3 / Do you agree or disagree with the answers? Why? What do you think is the Christian perspective on these questions? Can you support any of your answers by Scripture?

PURPOSE / To see God's intention for marriage.

SCRIPTURE READING / Genesis 1:27–31; 2:18–25

1 / Why did God make the woman?_____

_____

_____

2 / How did the man react when he first saw her?_____

_____

_____(Contrast 2:23 with

2:18–20.)_____

_____

SUMMARY OF TEACHING

As the climax of His creation, God made man and put him in control over all other creatures. The man's condition was privileged, but God saw that it was not complete; it was not good for him to be alone. None of the other creatures could relieve his "aloneness," and so God made the woman as a helper who was exactly fit for the man's need. Adam immediately recognized Eve as the one being in all of creation who answered his lack of completion.

The unity of the man and woman was physical as well as psychological. Because of it God saw them no longer as two, but as one. The intended result of their marriage was that they should "be fruitful and multiply," and create a family. Since that beginning, such a union of a man and woman makes them an entity separate from their parents' families. And today, marriage is still God's means of helping individuals meet each other's needs, and of providing homes into which children may be born.

This is not to imply that marriage is automatically God's will for all people in order to meet their needs. The Apostle Paul points out (as we will see in the reading for Day Six) that it is possible to remain single and at the same time live full and useful lives. But for the majority of people God intends the responsibilities and enrichments of marriage as a gift from His hand.

MAKING THE TRUTH PERSONAL

1 / What difference does it make to you that God established marriage and that it is not merely the result of natural attraction and desire?_____

_____

_____

_____

2 / What indications can you find in today's Scripture reading that God is concerned about you?_____

_____

_____

Thank Him.

PERSONAL REACTIONS / questions, commitments, prayer requests

SUGGESTIONS FOR FURTHER STUDY
TEXTS / Deuteronomy 24:5; Matthew 19:3-6
LITERATURE / Lars Granberg, "Major Surgery on the Family," HIS, Apr. 1974.
_____, "The World's Oldest Commune," HIS, May 1974.

10 Christian Marriage

PURPOSE / To see how the Bible regards the fact and fulfillment of man's sexual nature.

SCRIPTURE READING / Genesis 2:18, 24, 25; Song of Solomon 1; Hebrews 13:4

1 / What makes sexual relations right or wrong?_____

_____

_____

_____

_____

SUMMARY OF TEACHING

Christians believe sex is one of God's good gifts to us. He intended it to be many-sided, and every side is good. Sex involves a personality difference between fellows and girls, and means that they should mix together socially. Sex involves sex drive, which means that normal Christian fellows and girls will be aware of one another's sexual attractiveness. Sex involves sexual intercourse as a natural, wholesome, deeply symbolic act between a man and his wife—an act that expresses and establishes the reality of their union, both physical and psychic. The sanctity of sex and marriage is indicated by the fact that the Spirit of God uses the marriage relationship to describe His own relationship to His people: the love Jesus Christ has for us and His closeness to the Church, which the Bible sometimes calls His bride.

It is un-Christian to be ascetic, negative and gloomy about sex. Some people today hesitate even to speak of it. They talk about baseball, atomic physics, Bach, Jesus Christ, or the kingdom of God, but not about sex. This can give a person the notion that Bach is good but sex is bad. Nonsense! God wants us to appreciate His gift of music and accept sex as His gift too.

It's also possible to fall into the other ditch and become absorbed in the sexual attraction of people around us, like the Frenchman who said that everything—clouds, trees, public buildings, doorknobs, glass windows—reminded him of a woman's body. This is sex run wild, and is un-Christian.

If we feel as he did, we can count on Jesus Christ to help us change. Take dating, for instance. Too great a preoccupation with sex here will make us insensitive to a host of delights that God wants to give us as we date. The parked car becomes the sole objective, and in time symbolizes violent emotional turmoil and frustration. Godly dating, on the other hand, is careful not to incite lust, wisely emphasizing double dating and group dating more than single dating. And when the "going steady" period comes, a couple should be creative enough to plan interesting projects that give them the chance to get to know one another well.

If we're to have a wholesome view of life, we must have a wholesome view of sex. In His love God gave us sex, and He will teach us to regard it wisely.

MAKING THE TRUTH PERSONAL

1 / Why shouldn't you feel guilty about the presence of sexual desire?

_____

_____

_____

2 / Our society is becoming increasingly permissive about sexual indulgence. What precautions must you take to help avoid falling into such a frame of mind

on campus?_____

_____

_____

_____

PERSONAL REACTIONS / questions, commitments, prayer requests

SUGGESTIONS FOR FURTHER STUDY

TEXTS / 1 Timothy 4:1-5; Romans 1:21-27; Proverbs 5; Ephesians 5:3; 1 Corinthians 7:1
LITERATURE / Craig Glickman, *A Song for Lovers* (IVP, 1976)
V. Mary Stewart, *Sexual Freedom* (IVP, 1974)
Ingrid and Walter Trobisch, *My Beautiful Feeling* (IVP, 1976)
_____, *I Loved a Girl* (Harper & Row, 1975)

PURPOSE / To see what the relationship of Christ and the Church indicates for the husband's and wife's roles in marriage.

SCRIPTURE READING / Ephesians 5:21–33

1 / What are the respective responsibilities of husband and wife?_____

_____

_____

_____

2 / How does the comparison to Christ intensify the strength of the commands (vss. 24, 25)?_____

_____

_____

SUMMARY OF TEACHING

Marriage is an honorable relationship, part of the good plan that God worked out in creation. But its even greater significance is revealed when the New Testament discloses Christian marriage as an illustration of the relationship between Christ and the Church. This heightens the responsibility of a man and his wife to treat one another in a way that honors Him. Their life together bears witness before the world and their family to the truth about God's love and authority, and the obedience of the Church. No woman will have difficulty obeying a man who is willing to be crucified for her.

The Bible clearly describes the role of husband and wife. The wife is to submit to her husband, giving love, respect, and obedience to him. The man is to "rule" his wife with love, giving her leadership, care, and protection. Some will complain that this plan is neither democratic nor modern, which is true. Yet it is based on fallen human nature as it is. Christian marriage gives no license to the husband to be a tyrant nor does it reduce the woman to slavery. On the contrary, Christ's self-giving in love, and the willing and glad submission of the Church to His wise rule, is the truth that marriage must demonstrate.

Christian marriage is not experienced or set forth unless each partner fulfills his own role.

It is difficult to keep God's plan in view when society seems intent on denying it. Family leadership has often shifted from the husband to the wife, either by preemption or default—a major cause of juvenile delinquency and breakdown of the family. The voice of the wife should be heard, and her insights weighed; indeed, a loving husband will be anxious to know her mind on any important matter. But the man must be responsible for making the final decision, and the wife must submit to it. Christians should sense the need to uphold God's plan for marriage, to insure right order in the family, its witness to society, and the education of children in the truth.

MAKING THE TRUTH PERSONAL

1 / What bad effects are evident in the Church and in marriage when proper

rule and submission are refused?_____

_____

_____

2 / Why is it important for you now to prepare yourself mentally and emo-

tionally for your proper role in marriage?_____

_____

_____

_____

(How can your conduct affect your children's understanding of God and marriage?)

PERSONAL REACTIONS / questions, commitments, prayer requests

SUGGESTIONS FOR FURTHER STUDY
TEXTS / Genesis 3:16; Titus 2:3-5; 1 Peter 3:1-7; 1 Timothy 3:4, 5, 12
LITERATURE / Chip Stulac, "It Takes Two to Submit," HIS, Feb. 1976.
Walter Trobisch, *I Married You* (Harper & Row, 1975)

PURPOSE / To see what insights and actions are necessary to one who is looking forward to marriage.

SCRIPTURE READING / I Thessalonians 4:3–8; I Peter 3:7; Matthew 6:8, 33

1 / What does the Bible picture as important in your preparation for marriage (I Thessalonians)?_____

_____

_____

_____

2 / What does the promise in Matthew say about marriage, and the necessary priorities for discovering God's choice?_____

_____

_____

_____

SUMMARY OF TEACHING

Jesus Christ is our good shepherd and always works in our best interest. For many of us this involves marriage, so the question then confronts us: "What should I be doing about it now?" Various answers are given. Fellows sometimes say that we should ignore the possibility of marriage and become absorbed in other interests. They are often unprepared when they meet the right girl and marry. Girls sometimes seem to dedicate most of their waking moments to finding the "right one." Such girls are often empty-headed and uninteresting.

The best path lies somewhere between these two extremes. First, every Christian should study through the Bible to see what it says about the relationship between man and woman, and about marriage. Ignorance here is inexcusable.

Second, Christian fellows and girls should associate informally in the activities of the local church and IVCF. The duties they can perform for God can keep their friendships in wholesome perspective.

Third, we should date. If wisely used, dating provides a fine chance to get to know one another. Life is coeducational according to God's plan, so isolation from the other sex is unhealthy. A fellow who shies away from dates because of past immoral conduct will often intensify the pressures from which he flees. (On the other hand, a fellow who spends most of his time with girls must learn to socialize with fellows.) A girl who refuses to date because of a so-called broken heart will postpone her return to normal. On the other hand, a girl should not go to the other extreme and dedicate herself to finding a husband. Such a dedication thwarts higher goals. It may even thwart its own fulfillment, in that it produces ultra self-consciousness on dates and a certain inability to participate freely in life.

Fourth, we should try to get to know children. It's foolish to wait till marriage to learn something about children. Here the church offers a special service to students whose campus associations are boxed into one age group.

Fifth, we should cultivate our sense of responsibility. Marriage poses sharp-edged duties that vitally affect those we love, so we need all the advance experience we can get. We should volunteer for jobs and unswervingly see them through to the end. In short, we should cultivate the characteristics that will help us fit God's pattern for loving, thoughtful partners and strong, wise, tender parents.

Sixth, all of us should remember that God may have something in mind which for us will be better than marriage. Girls especially should not put all their eggs in the marriage basket and leave themselves unprepared in terms of a career—or for effective living in other areas of life. Enter into your major— and a wide variety of human relationships—wholeheartedly. If you graduate with no prospects for marriage, remember that it's not disastrous, nor is your life concluded. Enjoy your work or profession, become involved in a variety of worthwhile activities, and make your contribution as a single woman. Above all, be a person. Keep on growing as a warm, interested, responsive and responsible human being. Whether or not you ever marry, you'll always have to live with yourself! So trust the goodness of God's sovereignty in your own life, and let Him make you the individual He wants you to be.

Seventh, remember that two people cannot develop a sound happy marriage if they are disagreed on basic issues. Of paramount importance: a Christian for whom Jesus Christ is central will never find profound satisfaction if he marries one who does not share this same commitment.

Last, we should remember that if Jesus Christ wants us to marry, He is at present preparing our wife or husband for us, and us for that person. We must pray for patience, until His program of preparation is concluded. And we should pray for purity, so that we will approach marriage as servants of the living God.

MAKING THE TRUTH PERSONAL

1 / How can your current social life enhance or hinder your future happiness and success in marriage?_____

_____

_____

_____

2 / What are you doing to become a desirable and capable marriage partner?

_____

_____

_____

_____Read I Corinthians 13:4–7.

PERSONAL REACTIONS / questions, commitments, prayer requests

SUGGESTIONS FOR FURTHER STUDY
TEXTS / Proverbs 31:1-31; 1 Peter 3:1-7; Ruth; Genesis 24
LITERATURE / A. N. Triton, "Prepared for Partnership," HIS, Feb. 1973.

PURPOSE / To see why the Lord calls some to remain unmarried for His sake.

SCRIPTURE READING / Matthew 19:3–12; I Corinthians 7:7–9, 25–35

1 / Who did Jesus say should remain unmarried?_____

_____

_____

2 / What advantages are there to remaining single, and what conditions

make it desirable (I Corinthians)?_____

_____

_____

_____

SUMMARY OF TEACHING

Marriage is the will of God for the majority of His children. But some Christians are called to remain single for the glory of God. Celibacy is not the highest spiritual attainment, and marriage is an honorable gift from God to meet man's legitimate needs. But the work of God at various times and in certain places requires the commitment of those who will remain single in order to give their full attention to what is then most necessary and urgent (for example, pioneer missionary work overseas).

Their willingness to forego the joys of marriage does not grow out of a bitter or derogatory attitude toward the marriage union, or a lack of desire for physical satisfaction. Rather, it comes from their understanding that marriage brings many inescapable responsibilities that would divide their attention and keep them from doing an important work for the Lord. Nor does acceptance of celibacy for the Lord's sake imply that the individual will never be married. Singleness is a special gift from God to enable the called person to live fully and effectively without being married.

We should not regard marriage as the only complete fulfillment of human desires. If we refuse to find ultimate satisfaction in Jesus Christ outside marriage, we will not find it apart from Him within that relationship. God is still the goal of our existence, and marriage cannot fill the void that He alone will occupy.

We can be confident that God knows what is best for us and that He will not withhold any good thing from those who walk uprightly (Psalm 84:11, 12). If He sees marriage as a good thing for us He will clearly indicate that. Or it may be He will equip us to serve Him in an unmarried state. Both marriage and singleness can be rich with fulfillment in the will of God. Apart from Him, neither state will satisfy. We must leave the choice to Him.

MAKING THE TRUTH PERSONAL

1 / What kind of conditions might make it desirable for you to remain single in the Lord's service?_____

_____

_____

_____

2 / How would you regard God if He chose singleness for you?_____

_____

_____

Could you sincerely thank Him for it?_____Why, or why not?____

_____

_____

PERSONAL REACTIONS / questions, commitments, prayer requests

SUGGESTIONS FOR FURTHER STUDY
TEXT / 1 Timothy 4:1-5
LITERATURE / Margaret Evening, *Who Walk Alone* (IVP, 1974)
Sandy Flanigan, "Singleness: A Good Thing?" HIS, May 1976.
Alice Fryling, "The Grace of Single Living," HIS, Feb. 1973.
Dick Smiley, "The Fourth Sex," HIS, May 1976.

PURPOSE / To see what perversions of the marriage relationship we are commanded to avoid.

SCRIPTURE READING / Malachi 2:13–16 (modern translation); Matthew 5:27–32; II Corinthians 6:14–7:1

1 / What is God's attitude toward divorce (Malachi; cf. Matthew 19:3–9)?

_____

_____

2 / Where is the source of adultery (Matthew)?_____

_____

3 / What contradictions are involved in marriage to a non-Christian (II Corinthians)?_____

_____

_____

SUMMARY OF TEACHING

Because marriage is a sacred relationship that reflects God's character and affects the whole structure and nature of society, Satan tries to attack it in every way. A little damage done within the family weakens God's cause and enhances Satan's work greatly by obscuring and casting aspersions on the truth. (Consider, for example, the effect on children of divorce, or of the father's refusal to rule or love his household.) God set up a series of prohibitions to protect marriage—no adultery, no coveting of a neighbor's husband or wife.

The rejection of God's law has resulted in widespread abuse of marriage today. The modern concept of love as physical and emotional conquest for exploitation has led to a public denial of God's commands. With selfishness as the basis for a man and woman's relationship, marriage can have neither moral dignity nor permanence. Hence, trial marriages, multiple divorces, exchange of marriage partners, and extramarital sexual experimentation all lead to emptiness and disillusionment.

The Christian can have nothing to do with such impurity. And yet Satan has effectively clouded our thinking about fidelity because of society's pressures and our own selfishness. Even within the church marital abuses are regarded tolerantly, and there is agitation for revising divorce laws. Jesus reinforced the Old Testament Law's intention by extending it to the thought life, the motivation of our immorality. (We can commit adultery in church that way.) In marriage, as well as in the rest of life, God wants us to be pure from the inside out.

Some of us find it hard to believe that God loves us and will give us a good Christian husband or wife. And so by carelessness, or out of panic, we are willing to give ourselves to unbelievers. To do so is one of the clearest indications that we distrust God and do not love Him. We should prepare now by obedience and knowledge of our Lord to avoid marriage abuses later. Walking with Him will give us fullness of joy.

MAKING THE TRUTH PERSONAL

1 / How can your present discipline in refusing to entertain unclean thoughts help you avoid future marriage problems in the areas discussed today?_____

_____

_____

_____

2 / What else can you do now to make sure you will be obedient to God about marriage to unbelievers, adultery, and divorce?_____

_____

_____

PERSONAL REACTIONS / questions, commitments, prayer requests

SUGGESTIONS FOR FURTHER STUDY

TEXTS / Deuteronomy 7:1-6; 22:13-30; 1 Peter 3:1, 2; Hebrews 12:12-29; 13:4; 1 Corinthians 6:15-20
LITERATURE / John White, *Eros Defiled* (IVP, 1977)

SCRIPTURE READING / Psalm 104

"The heavens are the Lord's heavens,
    but the earth he has given to the sons of men."   Psalm 115:16

We live in a world where those who don't have, want, and where those who have, want more. This basic mind-set affects our whole view of life. Unlike the old Europe with its fading elite of ancient nobility, we have built a highly fluid American aristocracy of personal wealth. In this scheme, what a man possesses indicates his worth, and often his true character is overlooked or excused because of his financial achievement. And outside of this moneyed "blood," other men strive to improve their relative position in society by gaining and displaying various possessions. Of course, not everyone is so crude as to flaunt his wealth in order to prove his worth, but most people base their self-confidence in part on their material holdings. One of the drastic effects of a materialistic philosophy is the denial of man's spiritual nature and the consequent loss of his dignity as an individual made in the image of God. More drastic yet is the rejection of a need for God, and a refusal to bow to His demands. This is the end to which a wrong view of possessions can lead.

God has rescued us from living on the basis of the seen world and has shown us that nonmaterial realities are ultimate. This frees us from grasping onto things for security and meaning. But possessions remain a problem to Christians as well as non-Christians. Some react so thoroughly against a materialistic view of life that they conclude the material world is evil and having possessions is wrong. For them only an ascetic life is truly spiritual. Others look on material abundance as the unmistakable evidence of God's approval, and so are incapable of understanding poverty as a possible state for obedient Christians; and they expect God to reward them materially beyond their needs as a normal pattern. Still others, out of fear and selfishness, refuse to allow God to control their possessions and resemble unbelievers in their concern about them.

Since God has put us in a material world and has placed rich possessions in our hands, he obviously expects us to learn how to live with things. This week we will look at what Christian responsibility involves in the stewardship of God's gifts. We will also look at what effect possessions can have on our relationship to God. At a time when we are besieged by an unceasing stream of requests for donations to various Christian works, it is good to ask how and why we should share what we possess with others. And so in conclusion we will investigate some principles of Christian giving. By studying these topics, hopefully we will learn how to glorify God in the things He has made.

ASSIGNMENT

1 / To be done by the third day. List, in order of practical (not theoretical) importance, the basic motivations for your money contributions to God's work (e.g., desire to help where you sense a need, intensity of an appeal made, gratitude to the Lord, fulfillment of a pledge, embarrassment at not giving when others are present, personal interest in recipient, etc.).

2 / Make a survey of three Christian friends to learn whether or not, and why, they believe Christians should adopt the prevailing standard of living in their community. Then evaluate in a paragraph statement, telling why you agree or disagree. Relate to readings on worldliness in Unit Five.

PURPOSE / To see how we should respond to the fact that God owns everything.

SCRIPTURE READING / I Chronicles 29:1–19; I Corinthians 6:19, 20

1 / Why did King David question his right and the right of the people to give to God? (vss. 11–16)_____

_____

_____

2 / What was their attitude in giving (vss. 3–5, 9, 17, 18)?_____

_____

_____

SUMMARY OF TEACHING

We live in a world where men's positions and authority are often based on the amount of wealth they have accumulated. According to God's Word, this fact causes us to evaluate men wrongly (see James 2:1–9). King David was a very wealthy man, but he saw that his possessions gave him no right to be proud before either God or man, because God is the only one who can justly claim to own anything.

We are a part of the creation that belongs to God. That gives us a high value, and should cause us to regard every other man with respect because of his Owner. In our sin we deny God's right to our lives and we live independently of Him. By doing so we become slaves of sin and Satan. God has bought us back at the cost of His own Son, Jesus Christ, so He owns us doubly, by creation and by purchase. In response we must acknowledge His right to our lives. A true view of the world and men depends on our understanding of these complementary truths: God owns me, and He owns everything around me.

MAKING THE TRUTH PERSONAL

1 / Why should understanding that God owns all things cause you to be thankful for what little (or many possessions) you have?_____

_____

_____(How should it affect your

attitude toward the clothes you wear, the food you are served, and your friends'

clothes and cars?)_____

_____

2 / How should the truth of God's ownership affect the way you spend your

money?_____

_____

_____

PERSONAL REACTIONS / questions, commitments, prayer requests

SUGGESTIONS FOR FURTHER STUDY
TEXTS / 1 Peter 1:18-21; Acts 17:24, 25
LITERATURE / Ronald J. Sider, *Rich Christians in an Age of Hunger* (IVP, 1977)

PURPOSE / To see what God wants us to do with the things He has entrusted to us.

SCRIPTURE READING / Psalm 8; Matthew 25:14–46

1 / What things has God entrusted into man's keeping (Psalm 8)?_____

_____

2 / From the Matthew account, describe good stewardship._____

_____

_____How do the right-

eous servants use what has been entrusted to them?_____

_____

_____

SUMMARY OF TEACHING

God has entrusted the whole earth into man's hands, and we all share in controlling part of its wealth. He has also entrusted varying abilities and opportunities to each of us, so that one differs from another in what he has and is able to do. All of us are responsible to serve God faithfully in using the little or much that we enjoy in the time given us. We recognize the right of our employers to expect a good return from their investment in us. Seeing that God is our Master, how much more acceptably should we serve Him in our stewardship.

The Apostle Paul pointed out that God is not served by human hands as if He needed anything, since He gives life to everything (Acts 17:24, 25). But He is concerned about how we treat others, so much so that He equates our service to them as service to Himself. We have been loaded down with God's gifts: time, health, insight, money, homes, knowledge, goods, families, abilities, friends, love. What we do with them must not be a selfish matter; it is to be a stewardship that is part of God's working in the world. (How can we use the hospitality of our dorm rooms and social activities in evangelism? How is the Body of Christ benefiting from our spiritual gifts? What specific individuals get the bulk of our free time? What worthy activities are being supported by our money?) God will judge our use of all He has given us, including our knowledge of the gospel.

Our stewardship responsibility is corporate as well as individual, since we possess great wealth in goods and services as church bodies and as a nation. As members and citizens we must not only be willing to share our wealth intelligently for God's sake among the needy; we must look for opportunities to do so, in the same way that God seeks our best in all of life. (The question is not the politics of welfare programs but our willingness to share generously with those in need as a spiritual responsibility.)

MAKING THE TRUTH PERSONAL

1 / Who are the people in need on your campus (economically, intellectually, socially, spiritually, emotionally, morally)? List some individuals._____

_____

_____

2 / What has God given you to be used for their sake?_____

_____

_____

_____

What should your motive be in using your possessions for them?_____

_____

PERSONAL REACTIONS / questions, commitments, prayer requests

SUGGESTIONS FOR FURTHER STUDY

TEXTS / 1 Corinthians 3:10-15; 4:1, 2; Luke 12:42-48; Luke 16:10-15
LITERATURE / Michael Griffiths, *Unsplitting Your Christian Life* (IVP, 1973), pp. 81-93.
Ronald J. Sider, *Rich Christians in an Age of Hunger* (IVP, 1977)

PURPOSE / To understand the right use of possessions and to see why the Christian need not be anxious about having them.

SCRIPTURE READING / Matthew 6:19–34; Proverbs 30:7–9

1 / If God made all things to be enjoyed by men, what is His controversy with riches (vss. 19–24)?_____

_____

_____

2 / Why needn't a person be anxious about possessing things?_____

_____

_____

SUMMARY OF TEACHING

We lay great store in accumulating things, often without regard to their true value, and believe we find security in possessions. Advertising today reflects our thinking that enough money in the bank or in insurance policies will give us peace of mind and open the door to the good life. We picture that good life as a state of having all the material possessions we want and the opportunity to enjoy them.

God's view of wealth is totally different from ours. Not that He disparages material riches or regards them as evil. He is their Author, and has given them for our enjoyment; and it is possible to own and use any of them without sinning or being worldly. But God sees goods as servants, not masters; as aids in life, not goals. He knows that true treasures are not material and transient. Our attitude toward riches is corrupting when we set our hearts on them, because they become competitors with God for our allegiance and we end in idolatry, serving the created rather than the Creator. (Consider whether in your own heart love and obedience to God are a stronger motive than profit and financial security when you are choosing between possible future vocations, considering attendance at a summer camp training session, or planning your regular giving to foreign missions.) Love of riches leads to all kinds of sinning and moral blindness (see Matthew 6:22, 23; I Timothy 6:6–11).

Having promised to care for all our needs when we walk in obedience and seek holiness, God does not want us to disbelieve Him or become focused on gaining wealth. He knows what we need and can be trusted with, and He will give it to us. Consequently, we can be free from love of money and other riches and give our attention to eternal rather than transient values.

This does not imply financial irresponsibility for Christians. Good stewards will plan budgets, save for necessities, look for bargains, and make wise investments. But our goal in life will not be to possess things; and we will allow God the freedom to give or take as it suits His good purposes.

MAKING THE TRUTH PERSONAL

1 / Why is it possible that a poverty-stricken man could be more materialistic and sinful in his attitude toward riches than a millionaire?_____

_____

_____

2 / Are you setting your heart on riches and excusing it because you don't own much yet?_____What should you do if that is the case?

_____

3 / What reasons do you have for confidence that God will take care of your material needs?_____

_____Thank Him.

PERSONAL REACTIONS / questions, commitments, prayer requests

SUGGESTIONS FOR FURTHER STUDY

TEXTS / Deuteronomy 8:11-20; Matthew 26:6-13; John 6:22-29; 1 Timothy 6:17-19; Hebrews 13:5, 6
LITERATURE / Udo Middelmann, *Pro-Existence* (IVP, 1974)
A. W. Tozer, *The Pursuit of God* (Christian Publications, Harrisburg, PA, 1948)

PURPOSE / To see how possessions can affect our relationship with God.

SCRIPTURE READING / Matthew 19:16–30; Matthew 13: 44–46

1 / What major commandment did Jesus not mention in His summary of the Law (Matthew 19)?_____

_____

How was the young man's response an indication of his unwillingness to obey that greatest command? (cf. Exodus 20:2, 3)_____

_____

2 / How can material possessions destroy your relationship with God?____

_____

_____

What does it cost to follow Jesus Christ?_____

SUMMARY OF TEACHING

Some careful observers of American religious life accuse evangelicals of preaching a gospel of "easy believism," salvation through an assent to facts that do not affect the way we live. While some aspects of their criticism may be contested, they have correctly pointed up a misunderstanding of the truth about discipleship. Jesus made severe demands on those who would follow Him; He spelled out in understandable terms what it means to love God first, with all our hearts, mind, soul, and strength. In the case of the rich young man, Jesus put His finger on the things the man loved more than God. Because his possessions took precedence over obedience, he did not follow Jesus Christ.

We saw in Unit Seven, true faith is proved in action. Jesus asks us to prove the sincerity of our faith by giving up anything that stands in the way of loving and obeying Him fully. He mentions our loved ones as well as our wealth as potential stumbling blocks to discipleship (see Luke 14:25 ff.). This is a serious matter, since He says we cannot be His disciples if we insist on grasping our possessions.

Why then will we follow Jesus Christ? Although it is not an easy thing to meet the demands of discipleship, it can be joyous. If all our attention is fixed on the possessions we may have to relinquish (perhaps a career we had in mind, a comfortable suburban home, early marriage, or the American way of living), we may become bitter, and feel that the Christian life is a hard lot, bearable now only because of future salvation from hell and to heaven. But if we see what we gain in Jesus Christ, and all without our deserving, we will be like the pearl merchant in search of the greatest treasure, who was glad to give everything in order to possess that one incomparable prize. We can never hope to purchase heaven, but we can recognize that God, in giving us life and love in His Son, deserves all we can give Him. And all we forego will be amply repaid in this life and in the life to come.

MAKING THE TRUTH PERSONAL

1 / What do you know about Jesus Christ that makes knowing Him worth far more than anything you might have to give up for Him?_____

_____

_____

2 / What kind of material sacrifices might you have to make on campus in order to prove that Jesus Christ is Lord and you are His disciple (e.g., the comfort of privacy in housing, a budget of self-indulgence in clothing, hi-fi records, sports equipment) in order to share life with others, financially support needy

Christian work?_____

_____

_____

PERSONAL REACTIONS / questions, commitments, prayer requests

SUGGESTIONS FOR FURTHER STUDY
TEXTS / Exodus 21:1-6; Luke 9:23-27, 57-62; Romans 12:1, 2; 2 Corinthians 5:14, 15
LITERATURE / Dietrich Bonhoeffer, *The Cost of Discipleship* (Macmillan, 1967)
John White, *The Cost of Commitment* (IVP, 1976)

PURPOSE / To see why Christians are to give their possessions.

SCRIPTURE READING / II Corinthians 8:1–17; Philippians 4:14–20

1 / Why did Paul want the Corinthians to give?_____

_____

_____How had the Macedonians

given a good example?_____

2 / How would God respond to the gift the Philippians gave Paul?_____

_____

_____

SUMMARY OF TEACHING

The Old Testament states several valid reasons for giving. The pre-eminent motive was worship, to prove dedication and love to God. Both spontaneous gifts and those commanded by the Law were based on the truth that God deserves to be recognized as Source and Owner of everything. Giving was also based in obedience. A good Jew had to observe the numerous and specific rules of the Mosaic Law for giving to God and to others. The Jews also recognized their spiritual responsibility to maintain by offerings the Tabernacle (later the Temple), and the priests who ministered on their behalf before God. A final motive was concern for those in need: God had cared for their nation when they were strangers, homeless, and without resources, and they were to show the same care for others.

We do not find the motives for giving changed in the New Testament, but made even clearer. Now we see not only the awesome majesty of God and His sovereign providence; we see also the greatness of His love in the death of Jesus Christ for us. And so we give back to Him gladly our lives and our possessions, overwhelmed by His worthiness and our incapacity ever to respond to Him adequately. We have learned that obedience is at the heart of faith in God and of love to Him, and so we agree to His commands to give. (Do you share God's concern for world evangelism by supporting a missionary?) As we strive to become more like Jesus Christ we see that we can follow His example by sharing what we own with others. God is concerned for equality within the Church, and so we will give to those in need (do you know them well enough to sense their needs?), just as we learn the responsibility of ministering materially to those who have ministered to us spiritually (our pastors deserve more than handshakes and criticism from us). Finally, we are enabled to give our possessions to unlovely people in need because God by the Holy Spirit enables us to love them practically, and because we see that God now wants to work in the world through the Body of Christ and will show His concern for those in need through us. (Who is the Friend of publicans and sinners today?)

MAKING THE TRUTH PERSONAL

1 / How can you make the sharing of your money, hospitality, time, and ability an intelligent response to God's character and work?_____

_____

_____

_____

PERSONAL REACTIONS / questions, commitments, prayer requests

SUGGESTIONS FOR FURTHER STUDY

TEXTS / Philippians 2:5-8; 1 Chronicles 29:10-17
LITERATURE / Howard Guinness, *Sacrifice* (IVP, 1975), pp. 9-20.
Ronald J. Sider, *Rich Christians in an Age of Hunger* (IVP, 1977), pp. 58-130.
Yvonne Vinkemulder, *Enrich Your Life* (IVP, 1972)

PURPOSE / To see how Christians should give.

SCRIPTURE READING / II Corinthians 9; Mark 12:41–44; Matthew 6:1–4;
Luke 14:12–14

1 / Why shouldn't a Christian be afraid to give generously (II Corinthians)?

_____

_____

_____

2 / What is more important than the amount in giving (Mark)?_____

_____

_____

SUMMARY OF TEACHING

There was not too much question in the minds of Old Testament believers
about giving. The Law not only indicated when and what to give but also what
percentages of a man's income were due. The total turned out to be about a third
of his earnings. Beyond that he was encouraged to make extra gifts to those in
need.

Today we are not restricted to a specific form or amount of giving. But
there are plain principles to guide us. The New Testament fulfills other aspects
of the Law, and so we should not expect to find in it a diminution of godly concern for giving, but rather a refinement of our motives and practice.

All Christians should give to the work of God regularly, avoiding haphazard
and merely impulsive donations. Not even poverty denies God's child this
privilege and responsibility. (Are you still looking *forward* to being obedient in
this area because you're not "loaded" now?) We should give generously too, so
that specific need will be met and so we can prove God's ability to provide abun-
dantly for us. Though percentages are not indicated in the New Testament, it
tells us we should give according to our means. God is not concerned so much
about the amount of our gifts as with what they cost us; He is worthy of more
than tips. Gifts are not a substitute for other service that God desires; they are

part of our total self-giving to Him. If He doesn't have us, He doesn't want our gifts (see Psalm 50:7–23).

It is easy to be proud of our spiritual exercises, and so we are warned to give in secret, allowing no occasion for pride to arise. (Applause can be deadly.) Another healthy exhortation is to give to needy people who cannot repay (we won't be looking for rewards then), and to share pleasant things, not merely items necessary for subsistence (what kind of clothes do you give to the poor?). Because God has made us one we should strive for equality in the Church, using our abundance to meet others' wants. We never need fear obeying God's commands to give, because He loves those who give cheerfully, and He promises to match our generosity with His provisions to supply us for every good work. Small wonder Paul concluded, "Thanks be to God for His inexpressible gift!"

MAKING THE TRUTH PERSONAL

1 / Compare and contrast your condition and giving with the Macedonians' (II Corinthians 8:1–5)._____

_____

_____

2 / What value can a regular system of personal giving have for you?_____

_____

_____

3 / What needs is God regularly meeting through your resources?_____

_____

_____

PERSONAL REACTIONS / questions, commitments, prayer requests

SUGGESTIONS FOR FURTHER STUDY
TEXTS / 1 Corinthians 9:3-15; 3 John 5-8; Amos 5:21-24
LITERATURE / Ronald J. Sider, *Rich Christians in an Age of Hunger* (IVP, 1977), pp. 171-88.

SCRIPTURE READING / Psalm 2

Freedom from constraint seems to be the goal of both individuals and nations. People are throwing off a variety of yokes to assert their independence and achieve self-determination.

In family life this is seen by the choosing of divorce rather than responsibility when difficulties arise between husband and wife; by children's rejection of parental rules and authority when these don't suit their convenience. Because trustworthiness is disappearing, employers are increasingly having to establish controls to prevent workers from stealing company funds and materials, and to see that they produce the work they have contracted to do. Some elementary and high-school teachers complain that their function has degenerated from teaching to patrolling, due to the intractable spirit of their classes.

As subject peoples have decided to fight for freedom, various areas of the world have become trouble spots. Student demonstrations, peasant revolts, strikes, agitation for women's right go on because so many people have a sense of deprivation and a desire for self-expression.

While in some areas greater freedom is to be desired and applauded (such as independence for colonial possessions now capable of self-government or mitigation of women's near-slavery in some lands) much of the struggle for release from constraints does not result in good but rather in disorder and anarchy.

Why this upheaval in the name of independence? One legitimate reason is that people have been treated unjustly and want this injustice corrected. But another major reason is that individualism and self-realization are widely taught and highly regarded goals; and many have confused these with irresponsibility and rebellion. Similarly, insubordination has characterized the Church of Jesus Christ at times when believers have rejected the direction of spiritual leaders. The people have equated democracy with Christianity and used the vote instead of the Word of God to solve problems.

All of us experience the desire to run our own lives, make our own decisions. And so the question arises: what does the Bible teach about our response to authority? Starting with a study on the source of authority, this week we will look at the Christian's response to government, parents, employers, and spiritual leaders, in hope of answering our questions and producing God-honoring conduct.

ASSIGNMENT

Answer each of the following questions by writing a brief paragraph stating your reactions and the reasons for them (to be done by the end of Day One's reading).

1 / A Christian student has non-Christian parents who are fairly unsympathetic with his religious "binge." He wants to go to an important executive conference for Inter-Varsity officers and is planning to do so when a letter from home tells him that his parents expect him to be at a family celebration the same week end. What should he do, and why? Any alternatives?

2 / A student working as a server at the cafeteria steam-table is continually harassed by the unreasonable complaints and demands of her supervisor. One day another worker burns her hand by spilling some hot soup and is given an easier assignment for a few days. How should the Christian student respond when her boss insists that she assume the other girl's work along with her own, and hints that it was her carelessness that caused the accident?

3 / Although there is a fairly clear and well-known list of regulations for the men in a college dorm, and counselors ostensibly to enforce it, most of the fellows ignore the rules. At mid-year a new counselor, a reformer, comes to live in one wing and tries to get compliance by giving punishments. Finding a fellow (a Christian), whose bed is unmade for a whole week, he orders him to scour the sinks in the washroom every day for a week. The other men on the floor treat it as a joke and tell him to ignore it, expressing doubt that the head resident will uphold the decision. What should the fellow do?

PURPOSE / To see that all existing authorities derive their rights from God, and to learn how this should affect our view of history and human leadership.

SCRIPTURE READING / Acts 17:22–31; Genesis 1:26–28; Romans 13:1

1 / In what ways has God exercised His authority in human history (Acts)?

_____

_____

_____

2 / How extensive is the authority given to man? What is he to do with it?

(Genesis)_____

_____

_____

SUMMARY OF TEACHING

God, by virtue of His omniscience, omnipotence, creatorhood, and sovereign control of history, is the source of all authority. He brought all things into being at creation and then set man over the earth to subdue it and have dominion over all living things. All earthly government has been instituted by God, to maintain order in society, to uphold a standard of righteousness, and in ways not always clear to man, to achieve His purposes. Kings, judges, scholars, generals, engineers, scientists, policemen, parents, teachers, employers, husbands: all exercise authority and control over people and things within the will of God for society.

Men are to exercise control under willing submission to God, but from the beginning they have rebelled against Him. In this situation God does not withdraw their ability to subdue and control things, but their exercise of power apart from the Source, apart from His purposes, tends to personal and social alienation, frustration and death. Hence the spectacle of man's ever increasing knowledge and dominion (and potential to act for good) leading him to an ever increasing capacity for and practice of evil.

The Father has given all authority to the Son, and some day every tongue will confess that He is Lord. The Christian, knowing Jesus' true place, and both the goodness and terror of the Lord, calls others also to confess Him as Lord, knowing that only in slavery to Him is there freedom and life.

MAKING THE TRUTH PERSONAL

1 / What implications does the Genesis 1 teaching about the authority delegated to man have for your attitude and activity as a student and (potential) scholar or scientist? (What do you think is involved in subduing the earth? for you?)⎯⎯⎯⎯⎯⎯⎯⎯⎯⎯⎯⎯⎯⎯⎯⎯⎯⎯⎯⎯

⎯⎯⎯

⎯⎯⎯

⎯⎯⎯

2 / Since all authority is derived from God and yet much of it is exercised in rebellion against Him, how should you regard your human authorities? (Don't be hasty in your judgments; check today's conclusions against what you learn on succeeding days.)⎯⎯⎯⎯⎯⎯⎯⎯⎯⎯⎯⎯⎯⎯⎯⎯⎯⎯⎯⎯⎯

⎯⎯⎯

⎯⎯⎯

⎯⎯⎯

PERSONAL REACTIONS / questions, commitments, prayer requests

SUGGESTIONS FOR FURTHER STUDY
TEXTS / Isaiah 40:12-31, 43-46; Jeremiah 27:5-7; Daniel 2:20-23; 4:32; Revelation 1:5; Psalm 2
LITERATURE / T. C. Hammond, *In Understanding Be Men* (IVP, 1968), pp. 62-65.

PURPOSE / To learn the rights and responsibilities of governmental authority and to see how the Christian is salt in society.

SCRIPTURE READING / Romans 13:1–10; I Peter 2:11–17; Acts 4:18–20

1 / Why must Christians submit to governmental authority? List as many reasons as you find._____

_____

_____

_____

2 / What rights and responsibilities do governments have?_____

_____

_____

SUMMARY OF TEACHING

God has instituted governmental authority to maintain social order and establish rules for right conduct. Acting in the place of God, the state is to execute judgment on wrongdoers, approve those who do right, and serve the public welfare. People must submit to the government by obeying its laws. They must respect their rulers, pay taxes, and pray for men in authority so that all may live quiet and peaceable lives and come to a knowledge of the truth. To unbelievers the Christian's obedience to human authorities will be a witness that refutes false charges against him. In bearing witness to the life of Christ by godly living and concern for social righteousness, as well as by proclaiming the gospel, the Christian acts as salt in society—flavoring, preserving, irritating, stimulating. He knows that in civil obedience he is serving God, maintaining a clear conscience, and avoiding judgment.

The Christian must always serve God rather than men. Where a clear conflict between obeying God and the state arises, the Christian must deny the state to obey God. If suffering results, God approves the Christian's patient endur-

175

ance of it for righteousness' sake (see Matthew 5:10–12; I Peter 4:12–16). Where representative government exists, the Christian is responsible to use his civic rights to work for national righteousness (vote, write letters to government leaders, inform others, support reforms). Where the people have no authority, the Christian still must judge society on the basis of God's Word and uphold the truth.

Some fall into the error of a misplaced nationalism that places the state beyond criticism and overlooks immoral governmental acts. The Christian must never allow national allegiances to blind him to truth and righteousness; that would be to render to Caesar the pre-eminence that belongs to God.

MAKING THE TRUTH PERSONAL

1 / How well do you agree with God in your attitude toward traffic laws? in upholding dormitory regulations (quiet hours, cleaning rooms, use of phone, cooking in rooms)? in praying for the university president, the dean, and your dorm counselors?_____

_____

_____

_____How salty are you in society?

2 / Why isn't the Christian justified in being a political isolationist? List the ways you demonstrate your conviction that God institutes civil authorities?

_____

_____

_____

PERSONAL REACTIONS / questions, commitments, prayer requests

SUGGESTIONS FOR FURTHER STUDY

TEXTS / 1 Timothy 2:1-4; Isaiah 44:28—45:1; Habakkuk 1:5, 6, 12; Micah 4:10-13
LITERATURE / David Adeney, *China: Christian Students Face the Revolution* (IVP, 1973)
Stephen V. Monsma, *The Unraveling of America* (IVP, 1974)
Richard Mouw, "Political Evangelism," HIS, Jan. 1974.
Ronald J. Sider, *Rich Christians in an Age of Hunger* (IVP, 1977), pp. 131-70.

PURPOSE / To see what it means to honor your father and mother, and why God commands it.

SCRIPTURE READING / Colossians 3:20, 21; I Timothy 5:3–8; Ephesians 6:1–4; Matthew 15:4–6

1 / What responsibilities are implied under the head of "honoring your

parents"?_____

_____

2 / Are there loopholes in the command to obey? Support your answer.

_____

_____

SUMMARY OF TEACHING

The Scripture commands children to honor and obey their parents. In God's plan for society the family holds an important place; it is to demonstrate the relationship that God, the wise, just, loving, providing, guiding, and forgiving Father, has with His children. A human father stands in the place of God to his children.

Expansions on the basic Old Testament commandment to honor father and mother spell out dread consequences for those who disregard its intent. Death by stoning was the punishment for striking, cursing, or persisting in disobedience to parents. God's concern for the family was such that one of the prophesied purposes of John the Baptist's ministry, in preparing the way of the Lord, was to turn the hearts of the fathers to their children and the children to the fathers, lest He come and curse the land (Malachi 4:5, 6).

The New Testament likewise makes explicit that children must obey their parents in everything. Jesus excoriated those who refused to care for their parents' needs with the excuse that they had pledged their money to be given to God at a later date. St. Paul adds that one who refuses to provide for needy relatives has disowned the faith and is worse than an unbeliever.

177

Obedience is at the heart of honoring parents, but the command also includes respect and personal concern as well as care for their needs. As a caution to those who will make parents an excuse for not serving Him, Jesus says that unless one hates (in comparison with his love for Him) his father and mother he cannot follow Him. He is Lord in every relationship.

Occasionally parents will ask a child to do something that contradicts the command of Scripture. In that case the child must explain in humility and love why he cannot obey them. But there is more likely to be disobedience over the child's personal preference than over a matter of obeying the clear statement of Scripture. Some children presume on Christian parents' patience and concern for God's work, and neglect to give them the love, concern, and obedience commanded. Such disobedience cannot be excused by spiritualizing one's motives and claiming to serve God in place of honoring parents.

The command to honor parents is never rescinded, but when the child becomes a man, leaves home, and takes a wife, he then becomes socially and economically independent and the head of his own family. There he is directly responsible to God in his decisions, while honoring his parents and respecting their suggestions.

MAKING THE TRUTH PERSONAL

1 / When you are home, can your parents see that honoring them is a primary means of your honoring Jesus Christ? (How good are you at respecting their judgments? obeying their commands? honoring their position and their self-giving to you? Will they love Jesus Christ because of you?)

2 / Jesus said that religious excuses for neglecting parents were sinful. Can you think of specific situations where your busyness with friends, Christian activities or studies kept you from meeting their needs for companionship, news, or security in your love? Is your ministry of letter writing demonstrating Jesus Christ to them?

PERSONAL REACTIONS / questions, commitments, prayer requests

SUGGESTIONS FOR FURTHER STUDY
TEXTS / Genesis 2:24; Exodus 20:12; 21:15-17; Malachi 4:5, 6; Deuteronomy 21:18-21; 27:16; Proverbs 20:20, 30:11, 17
LITERATURE / Michael Griffiths, *Unsplitting Your Christian Life* (IVP, 1973), pp. 46-53.
Walter Hearn, "Bringing Up Parent," HIS, June 1975.

PURPOSE / To learn proper attitudes in serving employers, and the reasons for
these attitudes.

SCRIPTURE READING / Ephesians 6:5–9; Titus 2:9, 10; I Timothy 6:1, 2;
I Peter 2:18–25

1 / What characterizes a good worker's attitude toward his employer?_____

_____

_____

_____

2 / Why were servants to work heartily and with fidelity?   (On what did

their work reflect?)_____

_____

_____

SUMMARY OF TEACHING

From our vantage point as the most privileged working class in history, it is
difficult to appreciate the force of the apostles' teaching on workers' responsibilities to masters.   In their day a large part of the work force was in slavery, able to
claim few rights.   It was a group that well might have felt justified in rebelling
against its owners and overseers.

Commands to employees are based on the truth that God is Lord over all
and we serve Him whenever we work.   Each man must serve as if his employer
were the Lord Himself, treating him with honor and respect and giving him full
satisfaction.

The Christian's work is not a show; it must be done thoroughly and con-
sistently, regardless of whether or not the boss is watching.   In fact, the Christian
must do good work with a positive and hearty attitude, and not to curry favor
with the supervisor.

Some will object that their employers are hard and unjust men, that the workers have a right to get even by slacking off, taking company supplies and doing a shoddy job. The Bible's answer is a question: Where do you get the right to cheat God? Rather than complain and act bitterly, patiently bear suffering for the sake of righteousness and win God's approval. You can only do this if you see that you are serving Jesus Christ and not men. If you act contrary to the Scripture's rules for work you defame God and the Faith. By obedience you adorn the gospel and glorify your Father.

MAKING THE TRUTH PERSONAL

1 / If you are in school, your professors are your "employers." How do you adorn the gospel or defame God by your attitudes and work in these areas: (a) your comments on the qualifications and performance of lecturers? (b) attitude toward unfair tests? (c) quality of work done on assignments? (d) punctuality in work and attendance? Whom are you serving?

_____

_____

_____

2 / At the place you work, what distinguishes you from non-Christian workers? What should?_____

_____

_____

_____

PERSONAL REACTIONS / questions, commitments, prayer requests

SUGGESTIONS FOR FURTHER STUDY
TEXT / Colossians 3:22—4:1
LITERATURE / John White, *The Fight* (IVP, 1976), pp. 201-14.

PURPOSE / To see what responsibilities spiritual leaders must fulfill, and to learn what attitudes the people should have toward their leaders.

SCRIPTURE READING / I Peter 5:1–5; Acts 20:17–38

1 / How did Paul serve the Ephesians as a good leader? (Acts)_____

_____

_____

_____

2 / What commands did he give the elders?_____

_____

_____

SUMMARY OF TEACHING

In the unit on the Christian Fellowship we saw that the Holy Spirit distributes varying gifts to the members of the Church. God gives some individuals abilities that equip them to exercise leadership in the churches, and it is from these people that leaders are chosen and given charge of local assemblies of Christians.

The New Testament describes two specific officers for the churches. They are the elders (also called bishops or overseers), who are responsible to rule the congregation; and the deacons, who minister to special needs not cared for by elders.

The elders are sometimes described as shepherds who lead and feed their flock, protecting and strengthening. They must rule first of all by example in speech, behavior, love, faith, and purity; and the members are counseled to consider them and imitate their faith.

The elders are to bring the Christians to a mature understanding and practice of the truth. Their specific responsibilities include the public teaching of sound doctrine, preaching, reading the Scriptures, and watching out for false teaching. Having made plain the practical implications of God's Word, they are to oversee the conduct of their charges and encourage them to follow the Lord's pattern for living. Where necessary they must rebuke an erring brother and exercise church discipline. They lead the believers in considering the needs of the church and appoint qualified men to carry out decisions. In one congregation there may be several elders who share responsibilities and care for different aspects of the work according to their spiritual gifts.

What kind of response should the people give to their leaders? The Lord commands obedience and submission. The people must respect their leaders' lives and ministry and esteem them highly in love for their work. Because the leaders proclaim the gospel and bring spiritual benefit to the people, and rule by commission of the Holy Spirit, they deserve to be materially supported by the congregation.

MAKING THE TRUTH PERSONAL

1 / Why is it important to pray for your leaders? (What responsibilities and problems do they face?)_____

_____

_____

List three people in spiritual authority and what you will pray for them._____

_____

_____

_____

2 / If you are a spiritual leader, how can you evaluate your work?_____

_____

_____

PERSONAL REACTIONS / questions, commitments, prayer requests

SUGGESTIONS FOR FURTHER STUDY

TEXTS / 1 Thessalonians 5:12, 13; 1 Timothy 5:17-22; Philippians 4:10-23; 1 Corinthians 9:3-14; Titus 1:11; Hebrews 13:7, 17
LITERATURE / Jim Berney, "Do's and Don'ts for Leaders," HIS, Oct. 1973.
John Bray, "Flexible Leadership Can Save Your Chapter," HIS, Dec. 1972.

PURPOSE / To see the character prescribed for leaders in God's Church.

SCRIPTURE READING / I Timothy 3; Titus 1:5–11

1 / Describe the family life of a good spiritual leader._____

_____

_____

_____

2 / How many qualifications relate to organizational abilities? What is considered important?_____

_____

_____

SUMMARY OF TEACHING

In choosing leaders our normal tendency is to look for those with the greatest organizational abilities and put them in office. This should not be the case when it comes to evaluating leaders for God's Church. Technical skills must be there, of course, but Scripture's major concern is a man's character. We are not left to wonder what that should be. The New Testament gives two explicit lists of qualifications for elders and deacons.

Some may think that family life is a private affair, but it stands as proof of a man's ability to rule in the household of faith. The Christian leader upholds God's ideal for marriage. His wife and children are to be people of good character who submit to the head of the house, and their home is to be an instrument of Christian ministry through hospitality.

Because of his good character and behavior, the Christian leader should be well thought of by unbelievers. He should be one who is regarded by them as an irreproachable citizen, not quarrelsome, violent or quick-tempered, but approachable and humble. His life is to be moral and disciplined; he is to be temperate and sensible, master of himself in all areas. One evidence of no self-control, drunkenness, is clearly forbidden him. He must hold God's point of view on life because of a firm grounding in God's truth, which he accepts with a clear conscience. In contrast to a society preoccupied with possessing things, he is to be a man who seeks holiness, loves goodness.

The spiritual leader is a man reaching maturity in Jesus Christ. Not a recent convert, he has passed the test of living his faith. With his grasp of sound doctrine he teaches believers and refutes false teaching. He wins the approval of God and man by faithfully building the Church.

MAKING THE TRUTH PERSONAL

1 / Although an IVCF chapter is not a local church, the qualifications for its spiritual leaders should be the same. What provisions are made to insure that your officers are people of high spiritual character (in the choice of candidates;

in voting for them)?_____

_____

_____

_____

2 / Test yourself against the biblical picture of a good spiritual leader._____

_____

_____

_____

Would you qualify to rule in the Church?_____

_____

What is your reputation with outsiders?_____

_____

PERSONAL REACTIONS / questions, commitments, prayer requests

SUGGESTIONS FOR FURTHER STUDY
LITERATURE / J. Oswald Sanders, *Spiritual Leadership* (Moody Press, 1974)

what's next?

To continue your cell group and daily personal study...

Bible study guides

Getting to Know Your Faith
In this companion volume to *Getting to Know God* and *Getting to Know Jesus*, Paul Steeves leads you through a biblical examination of five crucial doctrines of the Christian faith: the inspiration and authority of the Bible, the deity of Christ, his substitutionary death and bodily resurrection, the work of the Holy Spirit, and Jesus' return. A valuable study for any person or group wanting to deepen their understanding of the faith. *paper, $1.75*

Learning to Love God/Ourselves/People
Richard Peace offers a series of inductive Bible study guides to help individuals or groups learn the meaning of love. These three volumes, each with five lessons, help you tie in your own thought and those of various writers with the teaching of Scripture. Comparing your written answers and discussing the "For Your Consideration" sections can make for good group discussion. *Learning to Love God, Learning to Love Ourselves, Learning to Love People, paper, each $1.00*

Learning to Be a Man/Woman
Kenneth Smith, in these companion volumes, shows what it is to become a man and a woman. These study guides point you—an individual, a couple, a group—to God and to the Bible. They don't make the learning easy, but they certainly make it possible. And what you learn is yours to keep. *Learning to Be a Man, Learning to Be a Woman, paper, each $1.95*

Decide for Yourself: A Theological Workbook
Gordon Lewis helps you to think through Christian doctrines in the context of many alternatives and to work out your own conclusions. It will be helpful if you can discuss your findings in a group. *paper, $2.50*

Young Christians in a Hostile World
Ruth Lichtenberger presents 25 inductive Bible studies on the entire book of Acts. These studies provide for us today not only a record of the past but a pattern for the present and an encouragement for the future. This is helpful to both individuals and groups. *paper, $1.25*

Books about your Christian Life

Basic Christianity
John Stott presents a clear statement of the fundamental content of Christianity and urges the non-Christian to consider the claims of Christ. *paper, $1.50*
Unsplitting Your Christian Life
Michael C. Griffiths applies the last six of the Ten Commandments to holiness in daily living, suggesting practical attitudes toward work, recreation and priorities. *paper, $1.50*
Sacrifice
Howard Guinness examines problems encountered in living in the Christian spirit of poverty, love and discipline. *paper, $1.95*
Take My Life
Michael Griffiths teaches us to avoid either a "tepid moderation" or a "one track fanaticism" by observing *all* Christ has commanded. *paper, $2.50*
The Fight: A Practical Handbook for Christian Living
John White looks at the basic areas of the Christian life—prayer, Bible study, evangelism, faith, fellowship, work and guidance; he offers refreshing insights into the struggles and joys of life in Christ. *paper, $3.95*

Books for background help

The New Bible Commentary: Revised
This is an entirely new and up-to-date treatment of the biblical text by evangelical scholars. It gives background information on each book of the Bible—authorship, authenticity, date of composition, textual problems, etc. It also contains a verse-by-verse running commentary. *cloth, $14.95*
The New Bible Dictionary
This book compiles fascinating information on Bible words, people, places, customs, culture, biblical introduction, history, geography. Like *The New Bible Commentary: Revised*, this dictionary is an indispensable reference book for any serious student of the Bible. *cloth, $14.95*